The Hitchhiker's Guide to

Effective Time Management

The Hitchhiker's Guide to

Effective Time Management

Second Edition

Christopher S. Frings, PhD, CSP

The only time management book you'll ever need.

2101 L Street, NW, Suite 202
Washington, DC 20037-1558

1 2 3 4 5 6 7 8 9 0   TCI   06 05 04

Printed in the United States of America

Library of Congress Cataloging-in-Publication Data

Frings, Christopher S.
   The hitchhiker's guide to effective time management / Christopher S. Frings. — 2nd ed.
      p.   cm.
   Includes bibliographical references.
   ISBN 1-59425-003-0 (alk. paper)
   1. Time management. I. Title.
HD69.T54F75   2004
650.1′1—dc22

2004046251

To my family who has always been supportive of everything I have tried to do or have done.

Contents

Disclaimer

Every effort has been made to make this book as accurate as possible. However, there may be mistakes in both content and topography. Use this book only as a guide—not as the ultimate source on the subject. It is sold with the understanding that neither the publisher nor the author is engaged in rendering legal or other professional services to the purchaser. If you require legal or other assistance, seek the services of experts who can meet your specific needs.

Your comments or suggestions are welcome. Please address them to the author:

Christopher S. Frings, PhD, CSP
Chris Frings & Associates
633 Winwood Drive
Birmingham, AL 35226-2837
Telephone: 205-823-5044
Fax: 205-823-4283
E-Mail: Chris@chrisfrings.com
Website: www.chrisfrings.com

For additional copies or information about bulk discounts, please contact the publisher:

AACC Press
2101 L Street, NW, Suite 202
Washington, DC 20037-1558
Telephone: 800-892-1400 or 202-857-0717
Fax: 202-887-5093
E-mail: info@aacc.org
Internet: www.aacc.org

About the Author

Christopher S. Frings, PhD, CSP, is president of a consulting and speaking company called Chris Frings & Associates, located in Birmingham, Alabama. A nationally recognized speaker on the topics of time management, managing change, reaching goals, and success strategies, he works with organizations that want their people to work smarter. As a specialist in change management, he offers customized presentations on problem-solving and increasing productivity during times of change. Dr. Frings is often called "the magical speaker," because he mixes cutting-edge information with magic and humor to create exciting programs for his audiences.

Dr. Frings has over 35 years of senior management experience. Before becoming a full-time consultant and speaker in 1987, he was laboratory director and senior vice-president at a large regional reference medical laboratory for 20 years. The author of more than 150 articles and four books, today he is a clinical professor in two departments at the University of Alabama at Birmingham.

Dr. Frings received a BS from the University of Alabama and a PhD from Purdue University. He is certified as a clinical laboratory director by the American Board of Bioanalysis and earned the Certified Speaking Professional (CSP) credential from the National Speakers Association. The American Association for Clinical Chemistry has honored Dr. Frings with an outstanding speaker award each of the past 18 years. He received the magician of the year award five times in Alabama.

Introduction

If you only do what you used to do, you get left out.
—Lawrence Killingsworth

Do you have too much to do in too little time? Do you have multiple priorities to manage? Would you like to free up several hours a day for yourself? If the answer to any of these questions is yes, this book was written for you. This book has four main goals:

- Sharpening your awareness of time and its value.

- Presenting practical strategies and tactics to help you manage yourself and your multiple priorities more effectively.

- Helping you motivate yourself to try the ideas in this book.

- Presenting ways to help increase productivity in you and your staff by showing you how to work smarter, not harder.

In Chapter 16, I'll ask you to try a 30-day plan to free up two hours a day.

This book was condensed from information I have been using in my time-management seminars and workshops for the past 25 years. It was written to help those who run out of time before they get the important things done each day. We are all being asked to do more with less. Managing time effectively—working smarter—and using technology appropriately allow us to do this. We must be flexible if we want to thrive in the 21st century's business world.

Because the book follows a logical sequence to working smarter and putting balance into your life, I recommend that you start at the beginning and read all the way to the end. I recommend that you not just read this book. I suggest that you study this book by underlining and highlighting the parts that are important to you. Go back and restudy the information at least yearly.

If you try the ideas and the 30-day plan in this book, you should be able to free up several hours a day. Even if you don't want to go that far, you'll find more than 300 tips on working smarter, not harder. You may be able to free up 20 to 60 minutes a day just by trying some of them regularly.

1

Many people never attempt to improve their time-management ability. It's easy if you tackle one time-management tactic at a time. Try one tactic, assimilate it into your everyday routine, and then go to another time management tactic. Some time-managment skills are easy and some are not. Don't dismiss a skill or tactic just because it sounds simple. Also don't dismiss a time-management skill or tactic because it isn't new. You may just need to reaffirm what you are already doing. Improving your time-management skills can make your life more pleasant.

Success comes before work only in the dictionary. Luck is opportunity meeting preparation. If you use these ideas every day, you'll find that you will be lucky more often and have more success!

—Christopher S. Frings, PhD, CSP

Why Time Management?

*What is time? The shadow on the dial, the striking of the clock, the running of the sand, day and night, summer and winter, months, years, centuries... these are but arbitrary and outward signs, the **measure** of Time, not Time itself. Time is the Life of the soul.*

—Henry Wadsworth Longfellow

Lost time is never found again.

—Ben Franklin

The phrase "spending time" is an accurate and precise one. You only have a certain amount of time to spend. We all have the same amount of time to spend each day we are alive. Spend it well. One thing's for sure: You'll spend your time doing something. The only question is whether you want to control your time or whether you want time to control you. When you don't take charge, time—by default—takes over.

Effective time management means that you work smart. Balance is the important thing. You will want to balance the following seven areas of your life:

- Mental

- Physical

- Spiritual

- Social

- Financial

- Career

- Family

These days everything seems more urgent. Because of technology, we expect everything in real time. In this information age, time management is more important than ever before.

THE KEYS TO SUCCESS

Success is a choice. My experience and research have both confirmed that there are seven self-management skills that are essential to success:

1   Have written goals.

2   Have a plan for reaching your goals and stick to it.

3   Expect the unexpected and have a plan for everything that can go wrong. Be receptive to change and learn to manage it effectively.

4   Don't make the same mistakes twice. Learn from your mistakes and successes and those of others.

5   Practice good time management by working smarter, not harder.

6   Get control of your bad stress.

7   Every day get a little better at what you do.

This book will address success strategies numbers one, two, and five. Goals are necessary for time management. Without them, you don't know what to spend your time on. Without planning you won't achieve your goals.

UNDERSTANDING TIME

What is time? Webster's dictionary defines time as a sequence of events, one after another. But my favorite definition of time is this: Time is the way we spend our lives. If you waste your time, you waste your life!

What is time management? You cannot really manage time. Time management actually means managing activities or events. Good time management means getting full value from your time. You can do that with the information in this book!

Why is managing time important? Time is our most priceless resource. You can use it or waste it. There is always time for important things! Start now for the greatest end result.

REQUIREMENTS FOR
EFFECTIVE TIME MANAGEMENT

What do you need to do to manage your time effectively? Two things. You'll need a system. And you'll need discipline.

This book can give you the first. You'll learn practical ways of practicing good time management. The second you'll have to develop on your own. Your commitment, desire, and attitude will determine whether or not you'll use this information to work smarter, not harder.

YOU'RE NOT ALONE

Think you're the only one who needs to sharpen their time-management skills? Consider the following statistics:

- According to a Harris Poll, people have less free time than they did a generation ago—37 percent less than in 1973.

- Seven in 10 Americans feel "rushed."

- Fifty-six percent of Americans feel dissatisfied with the amount of time they have for themselves.

- The average person squanders a total of 13 years in meaningless activity.

- Americans spend five months of their lives waiting for traffic lights to change, eight months opening unsolicited mail, a year looking for misplaced objects, two years trying to return phone calls, and five years waiting in line.

- Many people spend 20 to 30 percent of their time looking for things that have been misplaced.

- An Accountemp survey of personnel managers found that the typical employee isn't actually working 34 percent of the day, the equivalent of 17 work weeks a year.

- The average American has watched 18,000 to 20,000 hours of television by the time he or she has graduated from high school.

- Executives waste six weeks a year trying to find things. Because new technologies have increased the volume of information workers must process, they waste more than four hours a week—or 11 percent of their time—searching for misplaced, misfiled, or mislabeled items.

- Upper managers spend an average of 23 hours in meetings each week; middle managers average 11 hours.

- According to a 3M Company report in the Wall Street Journal, each year almost a third of all the people who use computers at work lose data. They spend an average of one week reconstructing or recovering their missing data. Nationwide this amounts to 24 million business days a year, valued at about $4 billion.

SIGNS OF POOR TIME MANAGEMENT

You'll find this book helpful if you are experiencing any of these signs of poor time management:

1 Rushing.

2 Running out of time before you have really done what needed to be done most days.

3 Chronic vacillation between unpleasant alternatives.

4 Stress and fatigue despite many slack hours filled with unproductive activity.

5 Constantly missed deadlines.

6 Insufficient time for rest or personal relationships.

7 A sense of being overwhelmed by demands and deadlines and doing what you won't want to do much of the time.

The next chapter will explore motivation. It will help you want to try the time management ideas in this book.

Chapter 2

Motivation and Time Management

The dinosaur doesn't exist today, because it couldn't change and it couldn't adapt. Therefore, the dinosaur became extinct. We will become extinct soon if we are not able to change and adapt!

—Christopher S. Frings

To increase your personal productivity and help you practice effective time management, you will have to change some of the things you are doing: You'll have to eliminate old habits that keep you working harder and develop new habits that help you work smarter. The best managers and leaders are "change masters." A manager's most important survival skill is the ability to anticipate change and identify new opportunities. We must all become receptive to change! You will have to make changes to improve your time-management skills.

I keep a plastic dinosaur on my desk to remind myself that if I don't change and adapt, I will soon become extinct. I've been giving plastic dinosaurs to my seminar and workshop attendees since 1987. Acting as self-motivators, the dinosaurs remind people that if they don't change and adapt, they, too, will become extinct.

DO YOU REALLY WANT MORE TIME?

Answer this question: Do you really want to work smarter, increase your personal productivity, and free up several hours a day so that you can accomplish what you really want to accomplish? If the answer is yes, now is the time to make a commitment to finishing this book and trying my 30-day plan for freeing up several hours a day.

As Zig Ziglar said, "Your attitude, not your aptitude, determines your altitude!" Having a positive attitude won't help you do anything, but it sure helps a lot more than a negative attitude. Practice keeping a positive mental attitude. That means giving 100 percent when less would be sufficient.

Remember the difference between efficiency and effectiveness. According to Peter Drucker, the father of modern management, efficiency is doing the job right. He defined effectiveness as doing the right job efficiently. Make progress in small steps, which I call dividing and conquering. Build on your successes. Remember that effective time management requires planning and flexibility.

Effective time management increases your self-esteem. When your self-esteem improves, our productivity increases. So when you get control of time management, the positive outcomes are increased self-esteem and increased productivity.

LEVERAGE

In every office, in every business, there is a huge amount of waste. The 80/20 Rule (also called the Pareto Law) says that 80 percent of the value is accounted for by 20 percent of the items. Learn to concentrate on the high-value 20 percent. Practical considerations for the 80/20 Rule include:

- 80 percent of your business comes from 20 percent of your customers.

- 80 percent of your profits comes from 20 percent of your customers.

- 80 percent of your headaches comes from 20 percent of your customers.

- 80 percent of your profits comes from 20 percent of your products.

- 80 percent of your results comes from 20 percent of your activities.

You get the idea. The whole concept of the 80/20 rule is leverage. A little bit of one thing generates a lot of something else. To put leverage to work you need to be focused. You need to be spending your time doing things that have a big payoff—not work, tasks, and projects that just keep you busy. If 80 percent of your business comes from 20 percent of your customers, why are you spending time on the 80 percent of your customers that generate only 20 percent of your business? If 80% of your profits comes from 20 percent of your products, why are you spending time trying to sell the 80 percent of your products that generate only 20% of your profits? If 80 percent of your results comes from 20 percent of your activities, then 80 percent of your time is spent on things that don't generate results. Eighty percent of your time is wasted!

The idea is to create leverage so that a little bit of work generates huge returns. What's on your to-do list? As a general rule, there are only a handful of important things—work, tasks, and projects—that MUST get done every day. When you get them done on time—and do them well—you achieve superior results, usually with minimal effort. When these tasks get pushed aside until a future date, they accumulate and stack up on you. What we typically do with our unfinished projects is think about them. We remind ourselves to do them, we look at the item(s) on our to-do list, we look at the pieces of paper on the top of our desk, we re-sort the piles of paper on our desk, and never get to the task that will only take five, ten, or fifteen minutes to complete. And we wonder why we're working so hard. We spend all of our time doing 'stuff' that has no value and no payoff, while the important work, tasks, and projects get pushed off until the last minute. This is what is called negative leverage. It's the opposite of the 80/20 Rule. Get maximum leverage by spending your time doing work, tasks, and projects that have a huge payoff. Complete the activities that give you 80/20 leverage. You'll reduce the strain, tension, and pressure in your life, and you will be more successful.

HOW MUCH IS YOUR TIME WORTH?

Many people say that time is money. That is true to a certain extent. You can put money in the bank and remove the money plus interest, but once you have invested an hour, the hour is gone. When you spend time on self-development, learning, and training you get it back many times over. Relating time to money is all the motivation some people need to want to improve their time-management skills.

There is no such thing as free time. We may have leisure time, but no one has free time. All time has value. People are often motivated to use their time better when they find out how much their time is actually worth in dollars. None of your time is free. How much is your time worth? Use the chart on page 11 to help you determine the answer. Put a price tag on each hour of your time. I suggest that you do this every year.

TIME MANAGEMENT AND STRESS

If you have too much bad stress in your life, you will get sick. If you are sick, you cannot practice good time management. If you don't practice effective time management, you won't achieve your goals. The secret is to eliminate the bad stress from your life. There are many good audiotapes, videotapes, and books on stress management. I even have a seminar and workshop called "How to Control Stress Before It Controls You."

You can do it! Make progress in little steps. Don't attempt too much. The rest of the book addresses the topic of using your time better. In the next chapter, you'll learn the basis of all time-management systems: written goals.

HOW MUCH IS YOUR TIME WORTH?

Yearly salary ($)	Benefits = 40% of total ($)	Total Yearly income ($)	$ Value per hour ($)	$ Value per minute ($)
15,000	6,000	21,000	10	0.17
20,000	8,000	28,000	13	0.22
25,000	10,000	35,000	17	0.28
30,000	12,000	42,000	20	0.34
35,000	14,000	49,000	24	0.39
40,000	16,000	56,000	27	0.45
45,000	18,000	63,000	30	0.50
50,000	20,000	70,000	34	0.56
55,000	22,000	77,000	37	0.62
60,000	24,000	84,000	40	0.67
65,000	26,000	91,000	44	0.73
70,000	28,000	98,000	47	0.79
75,000	30,000	105,000	50	0.84
80,000	32,000	112,000	54	0.90
85,000	34,000	119,000	57	0.95
90,000	36,000	126,000	61	1.01
100,000	40,000	140,000	67	1.12
110,000	44,000	154,000	74	1.23
115,000	46,000	161,000	77	1.28
120,000	48,000	168,000	81	1.35
125,000	50,000	175,000	84	1.40
135,000	54,000	189,000	91	1.52
150,000	60,000	210,000	101	1.68
165,000	66,000	231,000	111	1.85
175,000	70,000	245,000	118	1.96
185,000	74,000	259,000	124	2.08
200,000	80,000	280,000	135	2.24
225,000	90,000	315,000	151	2.52
250,000	100,000	350,000	168	2.80

My time is worth $_____ per hour.

My time is worth $_____per minute.

Chapter 3

Putting Balance in Your Life with Written Goals

The main thing is to keep the main thing the main thing.
A thing is not a thing until it's a thing.

—Author Unknown

GOALS

Fuzzy goals keep people from being successful! A goal is an idea directed to a desired result. Most successful people have written goals. However, most people don't have written goals. It's interesting that most people spend more time planning one-week vacations than they do planning their lives!

You can't score without a goal line. Goals are vehicles for making your dreams come true. A goal not in writing is a wish or a dream. Goals are the building-blocks of time management. Without goals, you cannot practice time management. Without goals, you are a wandering generality. With goals—and a plan for reaching them—you become a meaningful specific. Most people aim at nothing in life and hit it with amazing accuracy. Remember, you can't score without a goal line!

TYPES OF GOALS

There are two basic types of goals:

- Give-up goals

  Examples: Quit smoking, lose weight, stop being late to work

- Go-up goals

  Examples: Obtain your professional certification, become the manager of your department when the current manager retires next year, become the company's Occupational Safety and Health Administration expert

Share your give-up goals with everyone. But be very selective with whom you share your go-up goals. Share go-up goals only with people who will support your efforts to reach the goals.

CHARACTERISTICS OF GOALS

To be effective, goals must have certain characteristics. Follow these rules:

- Put your goals in writing. Writing a goal clarifies it.

- Make your goals specific. "Increase sales" is not specific; "increase sales by 10 percent" is. Similarly, "become rich" is not specific; "accumulate a net worth of $1.2 million by age 65" is.

- Make your goals believable. Your goals must be realistic and achievable. The test of a realistic goal is knowing what it will take on a daily basis to make it a reality.

- Make your goals challenging while keeping them realistic and achievable.

- Make your goals adjustable to changing conditions.

- Include your loved ones.

- Make sure your goals don't conflict with each other. If your goal is to be completely ethical and you cheat on your tax returns, you've got a conflict!

- Review your goals each day. Keeping them in your datebook organizer will help.

- Give yourself target dates for completion of your goals. Goals without schedules quickly become daydreams.

- Make your goals long-range ones. What you do every day to move toward your goals are objectives; goals are longer term.

EXAMPLES

When you're putting together your goals, it helps to see other people's. Here are a few examples:

- By the time I retire 11 years from now, I will have a net worth of $1.2 million.

- I will have my professional certification on or before December 1 of next year.

- Two years from now I will be the manager of my department.

- Thirty days from today I will no longer smoke.

- I will start making double payments on my mortgage every February, April, June, and October, so that I will have my home paid for in 10 years.

Remember, most people don't have written goals. It requires change and changing your habits to be a goal-oriented person.

FIRST STEP TO GOAL-SETTING

Before setting your goals, write down what you have ever wanted to be, have, or do, and why you wanted these things.

A Franklin Quest survey found that most people put the following people, standards, and principles at the top of their high-priority list:

1 Spouse

2 Financial security

3 Personal health

4 Children and family

5 Spirituality and religion

6 Sense of accomplishment

7 Integrity

8 Job satisfaction

9 Love for others

10 Education and learning

As you make your list of everything you ever wanted to be, have, or do, you might also consult the following list:

- Career

- Finances

- Religion
- Travel
- Health
- Personal development
- Leisure
- Social life
- Children
- Family
- Friendships
- Education
- Auto

MAKE YOUR GOALS YOUR OWN

The goals that you set must be your goals, not someone else's. Do not allow other people, such as children, employers, or spouses, to set your goals. At work, your company's goals and objectives serve as guides for your own goals. But it's up to you to determine what's really important in each of the categories listed above. After several days of evaluating the list, you'll want to shorten it to balance the following areas of your life:

- Mental
- Physical
- Spiritual
- Social
- Financial
- Career
- Family

BE FLEXIBLE

As your situation changes, so do your goals. Remember that your goals are only written on paper, not etched in stone. Don't feel that you are setting a permanent course for your life. Life is a process that changes constantly. As you achieve your goals, some things become more or less important. You'll want to change your goals to reflect your changing values, experiences, and desires.

In the next chapter, you'll learn how to put together a plan for reaching your goals.

Chapter 4

Creating a Plan for Reaching Your Goals— and Sticking to It

A good plan is like a comfortable shoe. It serves its purpose and flexes to accommodate the needs of the user.

—Michael Leboeuf

Goal-setting is important since it is the first step toward reaching a goal. But goal-doing is much more important. After setting a goal, the next step is to create a plan for reaching your goal and sticking with it.

REACH YOUR GOALS

Reaching your goals involves a nine-step process:

1 Identify the goal.

2 Set a deadline.

3 List obstacles that you'll need to overcome.

4 Identify people and resources that can help you.

5 List skills and knowledge you must acquire or use to reach your goal.

6 Develop an action plan and stick to it. Think "divide and conquer" as you make your plan and break your goal down into achievable objectives. It's much easier to stay motivated if you can visualize your goals in stages.

7 List the benefits reaching your goal will bring you. We all listen to the same radio station: WIIFM or What's In It for Me.

8 Commit yourself. If you constantly notice the sacrifices you're making to reach your goal, the goal probably isn't appropriate for you.

9 Visualize yourself achieving the goal. If your goal is directly and continually visible, your chances of achieving it are enhanced.

BENEFITS OF HAVING AND ACHIEVING GOALS

You'll find that there are many benefits to having goals and achieving them:

- You'll know, be, do, and have more.
- You'll use your mind and talents more effectively.
- You'll have more purpose and direction.
- You'll make better decisions.
- You'll become more organized and effective.
- You'll do more for yourself and others.
- You'll have higher self-esteem.
- You'll enhance your motivation.

COMMON STUMBLING BLOCKS

When people don't reach their goals, it's usually for one of the following reasons:

- Failure to establish clear goals, such as lack of written goals, unclear deadlines, and so on
- Failure to divide the plan for reaching goals into small units
- Lack of a plan or goal priorities
- Procrastination
- Fear of failure
- Lack of self-confidence
- Lack of discipline

GOAL PLAN TEMPLATES

The form, or template, on pages 22 and 23 should be helpful in preparing your goal plan. Feel free to make copies of these pages for your own personal use. Following the template are three sample goal plans. These are not my goals or your goals. They are simply models that can help you set your goal plans. Consider using the template for creating a plan to reach your specific written goals.

Once you've set your goals and started working on a plan for reaching them, you'll learn how to prioritize goals and use a date-book organizer in the next chapter.

GOAL PLAN

My goal is:

I will complete this goal by:

The benefits of achieving this goal are:

-

-

-

-

-

Major problems I must solve to reach this goal are:

-

-

-

-

-

Additional skills and knowledge I must acquire to reach this goal include:

-

-

-

-

-

People and resources that can help me include:

-

-

-
-
-

My action plan for achieving this goal includes the following objectives:

-
-
-
-
-

I commit to achieving this goal. I must stick to my plan.

Signature: _____ Date: _____

GOAL PLAN EXAMPLE ONE

My goal is:

To acquire a new Ford Tauras station wagon

I will complete this goal by:

June of next year

The benefits of achieving this goal are:

- Increased comfort
- Greater safety
- More reliable transportation
- More travel opportunities

Major problems I must solve to reach this goal are:

- Poor money management
- Low trade-in value of current car, which is not in good shape
- Higher insurance costs for new car
- Higher monthly payments
- No foreseeable increase in income

Additional skills and knowledge I must acquire to reach this goal include:

- Money management and budgeting skills
- Money-stretching techniques
- Information on how to get a good deal when buying a new car
- Information on how to get the highest price when selling my old car

People and resources that can help me include:

- Insurance agent

- Bank

- Family

- Part-time employer

- Library

My action plan for achieving this goal includes the following objectives:

- Record all my expenditures for one month

- Skip out-of-town vacations and deposit savings that result in an interest-bearing account

- Set up a budget and stick to it

- Listen to audiotapes or CDs about dollar-stretching and financial management while driving

- Take a temporary part-time job

- Put pictures of the new car on my bathroom mirror, on my refrigerator door, and in my datebook organizer

I commit to achieving this goal. I must stick to my plan.

Signature: _____ Date: _____

GOAL PLAN EXAMPLE TWO

My goal is:

To obtain my professional certification

I will complete this goal by:

December of next year

The benefits of achieving this goal are:

- Increased opportunity for work advancement
- Increased self-esteem
- Increased confidence in my future
- Higher income
- Great job security

Major problems I must solve to reach this goal are:

- Heavy family demands
- Lack of self-confidence, especially when it comes to taking tests
- Fatigue when I get home from work, which makes it hard to feel like studying

Additional skills and knowledge I must acquire to reach this goal include:

- Time-management skills
- Information about taking tests more successfully
- Positive mental attitude
- Study skills

People and resources that can help me include:

- Books, journals, audiotapes or CDs, and videotapes or DVDs from the library
- Employer
- Mentor

My action plan for achieving this goal includes the following objectives:

- Listen to instructional and motivational tapes or CDs on topics like time management, test-taking, and study skills while driving
- Budget time for studying technical material in my daily plan
- Attend seminars and workshops
- Limit television-viewing to two hours a week until I achieve my goal
- Secure my family's support
- Increase my energy by walking 30 minutes during my lunch hour four days a week, rain or shine

I commit to achieving this goal. I must stick to my plan.

Signature: _____ Date: _____

GOAL PLAN EXAMPLE THREE

My goal is:

To increase my savings

I will complete this goal by:

Ongoing

The benefits of achieving this goal are:

- Financial independence
- Freedom from debt
- Ability to retire early if I want

Major problems I must solve to reach this goal are:

- Practice of using credit cards for purchases and not paying off balances within 30 days
- Expensive habits like eating out too often, buying a new car every three years, and vacationing in faraway places
- Tendency to spend bonuses and raises as soon as I receive them

Additional skills and knowledge I must acquire to reach this goal include:

- Budgeting skills
- Saving skills
- Tips on reducing expenses

People and resources that can help me include:

- Accountant
- Banker

- Books, audiotapes or CDs, and videotapes or DVDs on financial planning

My action plan for achieving this goal includes the following objectives:

- Saving credit cards for emergency use only

- Make a list of credit card debts and pay them off one by one

- Make bigger down payments or pay cash for purchases whenever possible

- Put money from raises, bonuses, overtime, gifts, and paid-off loans into a savings account to prevent it from disappearing into routine living expenses

- Contribute the maximum amount possible to my company-sponsored 401(k) plan or to my personal retirement plan

- Find low-cost entertainment and vacation options by exploring my own area and enjoying local museums, historical attractions, and lectures

- Keep my car for at least six years before buying a new one

- Avoid lunches out and vending machine purchases by bringing lunch, snacks, and drinks from home

I commit to achieving this goal. I must stick to my plan.

Signature: _____ Date: _____

Chapter 5

Putting Tasks in Priority Order with Daily Plans

It's not where you start—it's where you finish that counts.

—Zig Ziglar

Most of us have many more things to do than we can accomplish each day. Unsuccessful people perform random activities. Successful people set priorities. Each hour you spend in effective planning can save you three or four hours in execution. You'll also achieve better results. By failing to plan, you are planning to fail. Put your goals and your plan for reaching your goals in writing.

PRIORITIZE

Prioritizing is the process of valuing. One way of deciding your priorities is to assign each task the letter "A," "B," "C," or "D."

- Priority A items are must-do's of vital importance. Items may fall into this category because of management directives, customer needs, deadlines, or opportunities.

- Priority B items are should-do's. These items are important, but don't have immediate deadlines.

- Priority C items are nice-to-do's. These errands, phone calls, visits, or other items could be eliminated, postponed, or rescheduled for a time when you're not so busy.

- Priority D items are shouldn't-do's. These activities have no real value, so you don't need to do them. One example is reading junk mail.

Work first things first. Spend more time on your "A" items than on "B" ones. By using this method, you will have done the most important things if you run out of time. Spend even less time on your "C" items. Don't even do "D" activities. Of course, today's "C" priority may become next month's "A" because of deadlines. A sense of urgency moves us to action.

Review your priorities daily. Remember Pareto's Law: If you have a list of ten priorities on your to-do list and complete the most important two, you will have completed 80 percent of your work.

DATEBOOK ORGANIZERS AND TO-DO LISTS

A datebook organizer is a calendar that allows you to write everything you do in it. It can be paper or electronic, such as a personal digital assistant. Everyone should have one—and use it. The datebook organizer is our tool for controlling events and activities. Don't leave home without it! Write essentially everything that you do in your datebook organizer.

At the end of every day, jot the next day's to-do list in your datebook organizer (paper or electronic). A to-do list should be more than a list of random activities. Make certain that it contains your daily objectives, priorities, and time estimates.

From the day you start using them, to-do lists will increase your productivity about 25 percent. They can help you:

- Set priorities and focus on important tasks
- Control your day instead of letting your day control you
- Get back on track after interruptions
- Organize your day so that you can handle specific tasks when you feel like handling them
- Take the strain off your memory
- Keep your desk clear by replacing reminders and other scraps of paper

Review your to-do list often—and always at the end of the day.

TIPS ON USING A DATEBOOK ORGANIZER (PAPER OR ELECTRONIC)

Here are some ideas for using your datebook organizer most effectively:

- Use your datebook organizer every day.
- Use the smallest datebook organizer you can that still gives you as much space as you need. Most people can use an organizer

small enough to fit into a woman's purse or a man's inside jacket pocket. I use an electronic personal digital assistant (Palm) that fits into a man's shirt pocket.

- Write essentially everything that you do in your datebook organizer along with your goals.

- Get rid of all your other calendars and use your datebook organizer instead.

- Keep your datebook organizer with you at all times.

- Make a to-do list in your datebook organizer at the end of every day.

- Plan your time by writing out plans for each day and week in your datebook organizer.

- Jot key points in your datebook organizer before making a phone call. Check off points as they're discussed and make brief notes as appropriate. This gives you a permanent record of your phone meeting.

- Identify different kinds of time, such as prime, sleep, leisure, decision-making, and travel, and schedule them. Don't forget to schedule leisure time. Leisure time is not a waste of time. Leisure time is necessary for lower stress. Plan your leisure time well.

Now that you're setting goals, creating a plan for reaching your goals, prioritizing, and using a datebook organizer, you'll learn the art of effective delegating in the next chapter.

Chapter 6

Delegating Effectively

Poor delegation is a major cause for lost time.
— James F. Evered

It is better to get ten people to work than to do the work of ten people.
— Traditional saying

There is no limit to what a man can do or where he can go if he doesn't mind who gets the credit.
— Robert Woodruff, legendary czar of Coca Cola

Delegating is a means of maximizing the number of things that get done. Delegating is getting things done through others. The definition of a good leader is the same as the definition of a chemical catalyst. A catalyst causes things to happen without being used up itself. If you don't delegate, you'll soon be used up. You'll attempt too much and spend your time in crisis management. Delegating allows you to take on bigger projects than you could alone and creates team spirit.

WHEN YOU'RE THE DELEGATOR

Use this process when you delegate tasks:

1   Select people who have the ability to do the job. Being able to do the job may entail additional training or a change in attitude about the task. Being a good delegator is like being a good coach of a football team. You have to know what projects certain employees can handle and what projects they can't. Hire the best people that you can. A sign on a plumber's truck said "Pay more and cry only once." This is also good advice for hiring qualified people. Hiring a new employee "on the cheap" is seldom a bargin and usually costs more than doing it right the first time.

2   Remember that the people you delegate tasks to don't have to do the job as well as you could. If they can met the job's minimum standards, let them do it. If you don't surround yourself with

the best people, you will end up having to do most things yourself. Provide the training necessary for the individual to succeed. The training could be self-study programs, cassettes or CD's, workshops, seminars, information to read, or individual training from the delegator.

3   Make sure the people you delegate to understand your expectations. Don't get bogged down in the details of how they should perform the assigned task. Describe the task's framework. Describe the desired results. Identify available resources. Discuss the assignment's length. Explain the work's purpose. Discuss limits on the employee's authority. Discuss how you will evaluate performance. Again, stress that you are more concerned about the project's final outcome than day-to-day details as it progresses. Provide latitude for imagination and initiative.

4   Ask the people you delegate things to to commit themselves to following through. Agree to a timetable and an evaluation plan. If you don't give clear deadlines, the people you delegate to may not feel accountable for completing the project.

5   Let the people you delegate to know that you will follow up. Then do it! Keep tabs on what you delegate. Balance the need to leave people alone so they can get things done with the need to monitor their progress and keep control of the project. For routine tasks or smaller projects, stop by occasionally to make certain that the people you delegate to have not run into trouble. For larger jobs, have the people you delegate to keep you posted in a mutually convenient way.

6   Don't do the job for the people you've delegated tasks to. Reverse delegation occurs when subordinates faced with tough decisions ask high-ups to make the final call. But a manager who starts making such decisions does the subordinates' work as well as their own, a common source of managerial overwork. A better solution? When someone you've delegated a task to approaches you with a problem, say, "Yes, that is a problem. What do you propose to do about it?" This conveys the message that responsibility for coming up with a solution lies with the person you've delegated something to.

7   Reward the people you delegate tasks to when they achieve results. Don't hog the credit! "Thank you" is a simple expression— yet it means so much.

Timing is vital! Sometimes the best time to delegate a project is shortly after a staff member has completed another project for you. Praising the performance on the previous task will generate enthusiasm for the new assignment. However, don't overload one person or overlook willing workers when delegating.

BENEFITS OF DELEGATING

Delegating will bring you three bonuses:

1 You will save time that you can spend on other projects.

2 You will signal to your colleagues and superiors that you are an effective time-manager and team-player.

3 Both you and the people you delegate to will see your confidence grow.

WHEN YOU'RE THE PERSON
WHO HAS BEEN DELEGATED A TASK

Use the following process when you're the one on the receiving end of delegating:

1 Find out how much authority you have for each assignment. Then carry out the assignment without getting approval for each step of the project's completion.

2 Repeat directions in your own words so that you and your manager understand the assignment the same way.

3 Request a deadline for the assignment.

4 When your manager procrastinates, write up a proposed action plan that begins, "Dear (insert name here), unless I hear otherwise from you by (insert date here), I will go ahead and (insert action here)…"

5 If your manager dumps everything on you at the last minute or overwhelms you with work, show him or her your to-do list. Ask for prioritization and new due dates on the various projects since everything can't be done at the same time.

In the next chapter, we'll look at ways of dealing with the tyranny of the urgent.

Chapter 7

Avoiding the Tyranny of the Urgent

It's the itsy-bitsy, teeny-weeny things that beat you.
—Paul "Bear" Bryant

Remember the saying "Lack of proper planning on your part does not constitute an emergency on my part." Strive for effectiveness. As Peter Drucker has said, "Efficiency means doing the job right, but effectiveness means doing the right job efficiently." Proper planning and prioritizing can help differentiate between what is important and urgent from what is urgent but not important. If most of what you do is urgent, crisis management will cause a lot of stress in your life.

You can't predict when a crisis will occur, but careful planning can alleviate problems when one happens. Expect the unexpected!

PARKINSON'S LAW

Beware of Parkinson's Law: Work expands to fill the time available for its completion. Don't confuse activity with accomplishment. Remember efficiency is doing the job right, but effectiveness is doing the right job efficiently. Strive to be effective. When faced with a number of problems, ask which are the most important and make them the ones you tackle first. Prioritization is the key. People who allow themselves to be governed by the tyranny of the urgent will have one crisis after another in their lives. These people confuse activity with accomplishment. They are always busy, but seem to be working on lower-priority activities. The tyranny of the urgent can greatly decrease your effectiveness.

A TIME-USE LOG

Can you account for how you spend your time? Most people don't know how they really use their time. Most time use is habit, and we really don't know how we spend our time until we try to keep track of it. Keep a time-use log in 15-minute intervals for one week to determine how you spend yours. Don't let anyone see it. It could be embarrassing! Start keeping a log tomorrow on how you spend your time. Then keep a time log for one week each year. The log helps you see how you can better use your time.

Before you start something, ask yourself, "Is this the best use of my time and energy?" If the answer is no, you might want to delegate it or just not do it. If the answer is yes, make certain that you have the proper skills before you go ahead and complete the task.

In the next chapter, you'll learn how to say no and how to avoid spreading yourself too thin.

Chapter 8

Learning to Say No

Skills are like tax deductions; we use them or lose them.
—Christopher S. Frings

Keep Pareto's Law in mind: Most of us can accomplish 80 percent of our objectives by working on the 20 percent that comprise our most important tasks. "No" is the most powerful time-saving word in the English language. Learn to decline tactfully but firmly requests that don't contribute to your goals. Point out that your motivation is not to avoid work but to save time so that you'll do a better job on your goals and your plan for reaching them.

HOW TO SAY NO

There's more to saying no than simply saying the word. Use this four-step process:

1   Listen.

2   Say no.

3   Give your reason for saying no.

4   Suggest alternative ways the person can meet his or her objective.

You cannot say yes to everything without spreading yourself too thin. Decide what you must do and want to do. Say no to all other requests as appropriate.

People who are always extremely busy often get caught in activity traps. They are not working on the important things: They are not making progress towards their goals. Instead, they are often working on other people's goals. Without goals, we fall into activity traps. We tend to focus on something. If we don't have goals, we focus on activity.

You may have to say no to a person to whom you report. Do you know how to do that? I suggest, very carefully. An effective manager will want to know when you will not be able to do what you have been asked to do. Don't whine about being busy. An effective approach is to express concern about having to neglect something else that they want done. Discuss priorities. Ask if they want to change the project priorities so you can meet the deadline on the new project—that is, "Which would you rather me do first or next?"

In the next chapter, we'll address the issue of dealing with interruptions.

Chapter 9

Controlling Interruptions

Your ability to communicate, persuade, negotiate, influence, delegate, and interact effectively with other people will enable you to develop leverage using other people's efforts, other people's knowledge, and other people's money.
—Brian Tracy

This chapter will address interrupters, drop-in visitors, telephone calls, and paperwork, which represent interruptions to many of us. In fact, many people put interruptions high on their lists of time-wasters. The average workday is interrupted every eight minutes by a phone call, drop-in visitor, meeting, or similar distraction.

Interrupters are people who want to shift your attention from what you are doing to something else. When possible, establish periods of the day when you won't tolerate interruptions. Then schedule interruptions into your day.

GETTING CONTROL OF INTERRUPTIONS

The first step in getting control of interruptions is to prevent unnecessary ones. Then reduce the time you spend on the necessary ones:

- Screen your phone calls, if that's appropriate.

- Make your open-door policy figurative, not literal. Close your door when you are planning or writing reports, for instance.

- Cut meetings or phone calls short by asking your secretary to interrupt when you give a prearranged signal.

- Keep a record of interruptions for one or two weeks, noting who interrupted you, when, and why. The form on the next page should help.

- Announce that there are certain times of day you won't take interruptions.

- When an employee asks to discuss an important matter with you, take control of the timing by saying something like, "Come now," "Come in 15 minutes," or "Come at 2:45 this afternoon." Of course, you must always find five to ten minutes for key people.

INTERRUPTIONS

Who Interrupted Me	When	Why	How to Minimize This Interruption Next Time

VISITS

Use the following tips when a visitor stays too long. Remember that tips that are appropriate in one situation may be inappropriate in others:

- When someone comes into your office, stand up and keep standing up. It's polite and will shorten the visitor's stay.

- Set a time limit at the outset. Say something like, "Sure, I can help you with that, but I've got to leave at 10:15."

- When someone drops in, say, "I need 15 minutes to wrap up this report. I'll come to your office then."

- Try working in an unused conference room, an empty office, the library, or the cafeteria before or after mealtimes. No one will know where you are, so you won't have drop-in visitors and other interruptions.

- When you see that a visit is going to go on longer than you expected, say, "Jim Bob, I thought this was going to be a short question. I should have asked you how long it was going to take. I have a 1:00 deadline to meet with my team leader. Can we reschedule this for tomorrow at 4:15?"

- Encourage appointments rather than unscheduled visits.

- Rearrange your furniture so that you aren't facing the door.

- Remove any extra chairs from your office.

- Close your door.

- Don't make unnecessary conversation.

TELEPHONE

Try these time-management tips for telephone calls:

- If appropriate, screen phone calls.

- Small talk accounts for up to 90 percent of many calls, so make an effort to keep it to a minimum.

- Learn to "cut off" calls as appropriate.

- Group your outgoing calls. Return calls from 11:30 a.m. to noon and 4:30 to 5:00 p.m.

- Keep pen and paper by the phone. Also make certain that your datebook organizer (paper or electronic) is with you.

- Say, "What can I do for you?" rather than "How are you?"

- Use an autodialer.

- E-mail and voice mail can decrease the number of full-time equivalents in an organization.

- Jot down key points in your planner before making a call.

- Let people know when you are available to receive calls and when you do not want to be disturbed.

- Use telephone banking or electronic banking to pay your bills.

SHORTENING TELEPHONE CONVERSATIONS

To keep your telephone conversations short, try these tips. But remember: Always tell the truth. Use these techniques only when they actually fit your situation.

1 Use a stopwatch to help you keep track of the time.

2 Ask, "Is there anything else we need to discuss?"

3 Say, "I have a long-distance call I've been expecting waiting on the other line. Can I call you back?"

4 Say, "A meeting I have to attend is about to start."

5 At the beginning of a conversation, say, "I was just walking out of the office and only have a minute."

PAPERWORK

According to Douglass' Law, clutter expands to fills the space available for its retention. Paperwork quickly becomes clutter and an interruption when not properly managed. There are five things you can do with paperwork:

1 Toss it.

2 Refer it to someone else.

3   Act on it.

4   File it.

5   Recycle it.

If possible, handle a piece of paper only once. If you really need to handle something more than that, put a check mark in the top left corner every time you handle that piece of paper. When you see three check marks, it's time to act.

You might find it helpful to separate paperwork into the following categories: letters, reports, files, and reading material. Then separate paperwork into three categories: items that require action; items that you want to read, pass on to someone else, or file; and items that can be thrown away and forgotten.

USING LESS PAPER

Use these techniques to reduce the amount of paper you use:

- Use shredded waste paper for packages.

- Make double-sided copies.

- Use stick-on fax transmittal labels rather than cover sheets.

- Use voice mail for short messages.

- Use e-mail to leave messages.

- Compose documents on the computer rather than on paper.

- Reduce the size of forms and eliminate nonessential duplicates.

- Circulate reports through computer networks.

- Learn how to use the copying machine correctly so that you avoid waste.

- Purge mailing lists of outdated or unnecessary addresses.

- Use the smallest envelope possible when mailing things.

FILING

An effective filing system is based on two important rules. The first relates to naming files. Don't use a "miscellaneous" category, because it is too broad to be effective. The second relates to the mechanics of filing. Put labels on the front of file folders rather than the back. Use staples instead of paper clips.

An effective filing system includes the following:

- Clear and simple categories

- An easy method for incorporating new files

- A consistent method for cleaning out files

Try these filing tips:

- Remember that you don't have to read something before you file it.

- Keep in mind that we never use 80 percent of what we keep.

- Organization is an ongoing process we never completely master.

- Toss things that you are comfortable tossing.

- File like things together.

- Keep a list of words you file things under, since it's impossible to remember all of the words.

The next chapter will address making maximum use of technologies as they become available.

Chapter 10

Making the Most of Technology

My greatest discovery of all was the discovery of what people wanted to use.
—Thomas Edison

From the .22-caliber rifle to the modem, technology has always helped us expand our reach and hit our targets more successfully. Your attitude toward technology is the factor that is most likely to affect your success. It's easy to feel overwhelmed by the introduction of new technology. But by paying attention to your communications needs and to new technology as it becomes available, you will be ready to evaluate any new device that appears to offer an economical and effective way to streamline your work. Technology is changing rapidly. To keep up requires constant learning and a commitment to never-ending improvement. Technology is just a tool and should be managed like any other tool.

In this section I will briefly mention computers, computer fax boards and modems, fax machines, telephone company services and telephone features, voice mail, cellular phones, e-mail, voice mail, videocassette recorders (VCRs), and audiotape players and recorders. By no means a comprehensive treatise on the subject, this section is designed only to get you thinking about how these devices and technologies can help you work smarter. No matter how low the cost, you should never buy any technology until you really need it. If you purchase it before you need it, it may be out of date when you really do need it!

You can determine whether you need a new technology or not by asking the following questions:

1   Will it reduce my expenses?

2   Will it increase my revenues?

3   Will it save me time?

4   Will it increase my productivity?

If the answer to all of the questions above is no, don't buy anything now! If the answer to any of the questions is yes, evaluate the real costs of buying and using new technology by answering these questions:

1   Is the technology very new or has it been around for a while? How long has it been around?

2   How much will maintenance and supplies cost?

3   How long will it take me to learn how to use it?

4   Will I need to continue using the old system as well?

5   Will I need to purchase additional furniture, phone lines, accessories, or other supplies?

6   What is the real life of the device under the conditions that I will be using it?

You should answer all of these questions before you purchase or lease any of the technologies described below.

COMPUTER

A personal computer (PC) is a necessity today. Get the right hardware and software. Since computer technology changes so frequently, any specific recommendations made in this book would be obsolete before the book was actually printed. It's easy to purchase hardware and lots of software you don't need. Always focus on the business reason for buying what you buy. Become computer literate. Take a short course or hire a tutor. After you master the basics, know how to find help when needed. It may be a friend or tutor you can call as needed. The help line of the hardware or software company may be helpful. There is lots of information available in bookstores, libraries, and magazines that you may find useful when you have a computer question. Consider using your PC for word processing, as an electronic datebook organizer, to organize your life, for calculations and spreadsheets, to track clients and customers, for research, tax preparation, financial analysis, and storing information, and for routine tasks.

PRINTER

Unless what you print is for your eyes only, use a laser printer. A laser printer is not only fast but also produces high-quality printing.

It's also quiet. People in the business world have grown to expect laser-quality print. When they don't get it, they notice and are often disappointed.

SOFTWARE

Appropriate software is essential for using computers effectively. It is now common for software companies to update their software frequently. Often there are "bugs," or problems, with new software. Frequently these new software versions are not even major revisions, yet they cost you a substantial amount of money if you feel you must have the latest version.

Before upgrading, wait until the bugs are corrected if possible. Good advice from my friend Dan Garrett is "Never use any computer software with a version number that ends in 'point zero'!" This isn't always possible, but I will assume that you get my point. Determine whether the revisions in a new version are major or minor. If they're only minor, you may want to wait for the next version before upgrading. It's expensive to upgrade all of your software every time revisions are made. Revisions are often the primary way for the software company to sell more software. If it wasn't for the potential sales to those who always upgrade to the latest version, the software company might wait until a major upgrade.

COMPUTER FAX BOARD AND MODEM

The ability to send and receive faxes directly from your computer can be a very effective productivity enhancer. A fax board for your computer allows you to fax documents from your computer without printing them out first. You can also receive documents through your computer fax board and print them out on your printer. A fax modem and easy-to-use software can increase your office's productivity. It also allows you to share computer data with other people.

FAX MACHINE

E-mail is replacing many faxes, and many companies are using fax machines less often. Fax as much as you can after business hours. You'll save on long-distance costs, and you won't tie up customers' fax lines during busy periods. Fax messages can save you money. You can usually fax a two-page message fore less than the cost of a first class-stamp, especially when you're faxing locally, using a WATTS line, or waiting until after-hours when long-distance charges are at their lowest. Delivery is also faster and more dependable, and the sender saves paper and handling costs.

Fax machines work best with a "dedicated," or separate, phone line. When installing a fax line used for business, make sure that the phone book doesn't list the number as a regular phone number under the business name. If that happens, your company will lose calls from customers and business associates who can't get through.

When you're buying a fax machine, consider the following features:

- Delay send allows you to send documents at a later time without an operator present. This feature will save you money, because it lets you send documents when the telephone rates are lower.

- Polling is the receiver's ability to initiate transmission or "pull" documents from remote transmitters. Polling is especially efficient when used with an autodialer after-hours or across different time zones as a way of reducing long-distance costs.

- A document feeder allows you to put multiple documents in a tray to be sent while the machine is unattended.

- An automatic document cutter automatically cuts the fax paper after a document has been received. Don't get a fax machine without this feature. It's a great time-saver that soon pays for itself.

- Group compatibility comes in three types. You'll want Group 3 fax equipment, which transmits a letter size of average text density in a minute or less.

- Purchase a plain paper fax machine. Thermal paper fax machines are dinosaurs. Thermal paper fades to an unreadable level in a matter of months. In contrast, plain paper doesn't fade or curl. Images are sharper. Operating costs may be lower. And you won't have to spend time and money photocopying thermal paper faxes onto plain paper to preserve them or facilitate handling. When it is time to replace your thermal fax machine, I recommend that you replace it with a plain paper fax machine.

TELEPHONE COMPANY
SERVICES AND TELEPHONE FEATURES

Telephone companies and telephones themselves have changed dramatically. Look for these features:

- Autodialers store numbers you call frequently. To make a call, you just push one or two code numbers. An autodialer can save you time if you make a lot of calls to the same numbers. Autodialers are built into many phones and fax machines, but stand-alone autodialers are available at low cost.

- Automatic redial allows you to redial the last number you dialed by pushing the redial button. This feature can save you time.

- Cordless phones allow you to continue a conversation while walking about your office or building. That means you can do other things while you talk.

- Speaker phones let you talk to someone without holding the phone in your hand. This frees you to do other things while you talk.

- Call forwarding automatically forwards your calls to another number you have designated.

- Call waiting signals that someone is trying to reach you while you are on another call. I do not recommend this feature for business lines. During a business call, it's rude to ask the person you're talking to to hold on while you see who's calling.

- Telephone answering machines take your calls when you are out. Change the message often to reflect whether you are in or out of the office, when you will be available to receive calls, when you plan to return calls, and so on.

- "Memory Call" is a telephone answering service that works even when your line is busy. Available from many local phone companies, it's a great feature at low cost! It's actually voice mail.

CELLULAR PHONES

Cellular phones have been shown to help efficiency and reduce stress for commuters. However, people who use a cellular phone while driving also have more automobile accidents because they're distracted. To be a safer cellular phone user, pull over to a safe place before you place a call. If you receive a call while driving, always use a hands-free speakerphone so that you can concentrate on the road. Take notes only when your car is parked.

Cellular phones aren't only dangerous for their users. Watch for signs asking you to turn off two-way radios in blasting areas. Turn off your phone, because an incoming call could cause the phone to transmit and inadvertently set off a premature explosion! It is also against Federal Communications Commission and Federal Aviation Administration regulations to use a cellular phone on planes. Your phone must be turned off, because cellular phones may interfere with the plane's communication and navigation systems.

THE INFORMATION SUPERHIGHWAY

Don't be left behind on the information superhighway: Use an on-line service to connect with the future now. It's easy to hop on board. For a modest monthly fee, you can have access to e-mail and hundreds of other services. Simply attach a modem to your PC and sign up with any of the Internet service providers. Most provide free or low-cost sign-up kits obtainable from the providers or computer stores. You can use e-mail to send information to anyone else who has e-mail capability, even if that person uses a different system than you. This happens through the Internet, a worldwide network of linked computers that allows you to send e-mail and files to millions of people. Happy surfing in cyberspace!

ELECTRONIC MAIL (E-MAIL)

Commercial Internet Service Providers (ISPs) like ATT Worldnet, America Online, and Mindspring all include e-mail features that allow you to communicate with other people no matter what service they use. Sending and receiving e-mail is the number-one reason people use on-line services. E-mail is second only to the telephone as a way to keep in touch.

You can be overwhelmed by e-mail. E-mail increases efficiency by reducing the need for secretaries to answer phone calls and write memos. It's a fast, cost-effective alternative to paper mail, because it's transmitted instantly. There's no waiting for the U.S. Postal Service. E-mail is also more reliable than faxing. Your e-mail messages can't get stuck in the fax machine, can't be clipped to the wrong cover sheet and sent to the wrong person, can't get lost in a pile of papers, and can't be read by others.

When you use e-mail, you must change your writing style to reflect this speedy form of communication. Computer monitors are harder on the eyes than paper, so give your readers a reason to read your e-mail and let them off the hook quickly. Use these tips:

- Identify your purpose for writing immediately, either in the subject box or in the first paragraph. Keep your reader's attention, by being short and specific.

- Give your reader the main idea first. If background information is necessary, give it after the main idea.

- Make your message easy on the eye and the brain. Use short sentences and bullet points. Leave space between paragraphs. Don't type everything upper case, because it's hard to read if it's longer than one or two lines.

- When you have to write a long or complicated message, suggest to the reader in the first paragraph that he or she print out a hard copy to read. It's much easier to read a long document on paper than on a computer monitor.

- Reread your message before sending and check for mistakes and clarity. Ask yourself whether you would grasp the idea on first reading if you received this message. If not, fix it!

- Save an electronic copy of your e-mail messages for your files.

You should also keep legal and other considerations in mind. E-mail messages placed on computer bulletin boards are considered published, so they may be deemed libelous. Be careful what you write! Don't use e-mail to send highly sensitive messages, proprietary messages, or messages that could be interpreted as a breach of patient confidentiality. Attorneys increasingly demand production of e-mail messages during legal discovery proceedings to build malpractice cases. Use the same caution in drafting e-mail messages you use when writing a formal letter. Never include offensive, obscene, discriminatory, or ill-considered remarks.

VOICE MAIL

Voice mail (VM) is the system of automatic answering machines that has become part of many company telephone systems. Its main advantage is its ability to deliver an accurate message to someone without having to wait to actually speak to the individual personally. If used correctly, voice mail greatly enhances the efficiency and productivity of all employees. It reduces the need for operators and secretaries to handle calls and take messages, which lowers labor costs. It eliminates the need to return many phone calls. It lets you leave multiple messages with one call. It shortens calls by eliminating chit-chat. It reduces the need to put callers on hold. And it lets people stay in contact outside of normal business hours. When used poorly, however, voice mail alienates your callers.

Whenever I want to leave a message for someone I know, and that person isn't in, I frequently ask the person answering the phone if I can leave a message on VM. That way I know that an error won't creep in and the message will not be filtered through someone else's mind.

Some companies have a long way to go to get the most from their voice-mail systems. But if we all practice etiquette and common courtesy, voice mail can be an effective business communications tool. Use the tips below to get the most out of your voice-mail system. Think of VM as a substitute for writing a letter. Anything you can do in a letter you can also do in VM.

- Record your outgoing message in your own voice and update it frequently with personal, informational messages. Don't say, "I'm not able to come to the phone right now." That's obvious! The message should be accurate, brief, clear, and up to date. An outdated greeting shows a lack of concern.

- The recording should name an alternative person to speak to if the desired person isn't available.

- If you frequently check your voice mail for messages, say so in your message. People want to know how long it will be before you get their messages.

- Make sure to change your message when you are out of town. You could lose an important client by not calling back for several days or even weeks.

- Return all calls or ask someone to return them on your behalf.

- Don't have a long menu up front that the caller must work through. This can be time consuming and frustrating to your callers. At most, have four options.

Using voice mail improperly can hurt your business. Don't make these common mistakes:

- Lengthy menus: Menus should be short and to the point. They should also give the caller the option of speaking promptly to a live person.

- Equating voice-mail systems with answering machines: Voice mail is often underestimated. An answering machine can't answer a phone when the line is busy nor can it forward a message to another employee as most voice-mail systems can. Voice-mail messages can also be sent to several people at the same time.

- Letting employees hide behind their voice mail: Some people hide behind their voice mail, using it as a screen. They stop answering their phones, forcing callers to leave messages, and then return only those calls they wish to return. This can be bad for business, especially if yours is a service business.

- Failing to train employees to use voice mail effectively: People should be taught how to leave clear messages; change messages when they're in meetings or on business trips or vacation; and name an alternate person who can take their calls.

- Failing to inform key clients about your voice-mail system: Since there is still some resistance to voice mail, letting people know ahead of time that you are installing voice mail and explaining why you're doing it will help to overcome that resistance.

Of course, sometimes you'll be on the other side of the voice-mail system. Use these tips to make the most of other people's systems:

- Bypass the initial recording when needed. Many systems allow you to bypass the recording by pushing "0." Jot down frequently used extensions in your address book or rotary card file. Most systems allow you to reach your party you call in seconds.

- Leave a complete, detailed message. Ask for any information that you need. That way the other person can get the ball rolling before he or she calls you back.

- Learn from other people's mistakes. Make a note of what they're doing wrong and what irritates you about their systems. Be certain that you don't make the same mistakes.

VIDEOCASSETTE RECORDER (VCR)

Use a VCR to watch instructional and motivational programs. Or use it to record television programs that you want to watch. Play them back when it's convenient for you and fast forward through the commercials. You'll save time: You can watch a 60-minute program in approximately 47 minutes by using this technique!

AUDIOCASSETTE PLAYER AND RECORDER

An audiocassette player and recorder or a compact disk (CD) player lets you listen to instructional and motivational audiotapes or CDs while traveling. Motivational tapes are a great way to stay motivated; books on tape, educational tapes, and training tapes are a great way to learn something new. You can also use your recorder to tape your presentations, both formal and informal. Listening to them later will help you give better presentations.

Now that you've thought about how technology can help you use your time more effectively, you'll learn how to address the issue of excellence vs. perfection in the next chapter.

Chapter 11

Avoiding Perfectionism While Striving for Excellence

Only a mediocre person is always at their best.

—Somerset Maugham

Striving for perfection frequently costs us more than the increased benefits justify. In some elementary and high schools, there is a tendency to expect perfection from the students: 100 percent of the words spelled correctly, no typographical errors in term papers, no math errors, and so on. There is a difference between striving for excellence and striving for perfection. Excellence is attainable, gratifying, and healthy. Perfection is often unattainable and causes frustration. We all want to do the job right. None of us is perfect. When you expect perfection in yourself and in others, you make a large mistake. Perfection can immobilize us to a large extent— always trying to do things better and better until we reach a point where it's impossible to do things better.

Perfectionists frequently have low productivity, because they don't want to do it if it isn't perfect. Since it isn't perfect, nothing gets done. You can't make a mistake if you do nothing. However, doing nothing is a mistake!

At times the pursuit of perfection is OK! It's all right to strive for perfection when you're performing a medical laboratory test, filing your tax return, building a bridge, or programming a computer. However, most of us apply perfectionism inappropriately. Perfectionism isn't necessary for most of what we do. Being a perfectionist about your car, your spouse, your clothes, your employees, and so forth is a waste of time. This failed perfectionism can actually keep you from achieving your high-priority goals, because you are working on the wrong things—perfectionism where perfectionism isn't necessary or even achievable.

People who expect perfection are frequently poor delegators. They won't allow mistakes, and therefore they are reluctant to delegate.

When perfection is essential, do your best to deliver it.

The next chapter will help you control another common problem: procrastination.

Chapter 12

Controlling Procrastination

When we identify the problem, we have taken a major step toward solving it.
—Zig Ziglar

Visualize the end result of an activity rather than the activity itself. Divide and conquer by breaking the big task into smaller units. Clear the clutter! Establish an environment that is conducive to getting the job done. Use to-do lists effectively.

Procrastination is defined as putting things off or delaying doing something until later. The definition does not associate negativity with the word, nor should it necessarily. Procrastination is one way a person protects him or herself from mental or physical discomfort. Procrastination is the habit of indecision. Everyone procrastinates to some degree. Procrastination is a learned experience. Procrastination is normal! However, when procrastination affects your performance or productivity seriously, you need to control it.

Too many people spend too much time "beginning to begin to begin to commence to get started." They spend so much time preparing to do something that they often run out of time to do it. This is a form of procrastination—that is, using lengthy planning as a procrastination tool.

REASONS FOR PROCRASTINATION

The reasons why we procrastinate include the following:

- We fear failure.

- We don't want to do something.

- The task is too big.

- The task is not high on our list of priorities.

EXAMINING YOUR PROCRASTINATION HABITS

The first step toward controlling procrastination is to examine your procrastination habits. You will want to delve into your personal history of what, when, why, and how you procrastinate. This will help you get a handle on what kinds of things you procrastinate on, how often, and why. The following techniques will help you examine your procrastination habits:

- Keep a personal log for several weeks and record each episode of procrastination. The form on the next page should help.

- Use your log to note the tasks you procrastinated on, why you procrastinated, and which of the following strategies you could use to eliminate procrastination in similar situations in the future.

Don't let anyone see your log.

Procrastination Record

What I Procrastinated On	Why	How to Minimize This Next Time

TIPS FOR CONTROLLING PROCRASTINATION

The following strategies can help you control procrastination:

- Clear the clutter. Clutter distracts you from the task you should be doing. When distracted, we tend to do things that we want to do as opposed to things we should do. A cluttered desk is an interruption every time you try to use it or find anything on it.

- Establish an environment that is conducive to getting the job done. Ask yourself, "What is the best time and place to do this job?"

- Use to-do lists effectively. A to-do list that has been prioritized with a deadline and noted in your datebook organizer is a useful way of controlling procrastination.

- Divide and conquer. Divide the big task into a number of small jobs and set deadlines for each of them. Before you know it, you will have the big task completed.

- Picture the end result of the finished job. Visualizing the positive aspects of completing a task may help you commit to doing it. If it is an unpleasant job, remember that when you have completed it you can go on to something more pleasant.

- Reward yourself. Give yourself a reward when you complete the task you are procrastinating on. Be sure not to reward yourself until the task is completed.

- Controlling procrastination requires self-analysis, which may cause you some discomfort. Don't procrastinate on getting started on the project of controlling procrastination. Don't put it off! Include controlling procrastination in your goals, write it in your datebook organizer, and give it a priority. Start today.

In the next chapter, you'll learn how to hold effective meetings.

Chapter 13

Holding Efficient Meetings

Show me a person who likes to go to meetings, and I'll show you a person who doesn't have enough to do.
—Joe Griffith

A meeting is when two or more people come together to discuss something. Usually it implies a face-to-face meeting, but could be a telephone meeting or an electronic (videoconferencing) meeting. How many times have you been in a meeting thinking, "What a waste of time? I could have accomplished more doing other things instead of being at this meeting."? This chapter will give you a formula for more effective meetings. The cost of meetings is high. Since middle managers average 11 hours a week in meetings, and upper managers average 23 hours per week in meetings, it is important that we master the skill of holding effective meetings. Conducting a meeting well is both science and art. Conducting good meetings is a learned skill. Holding an effective meeting is one more way to work smarter, not harder!

SHOULD YOU HOLD A MEETING?

The first question to ask when deciding whether to hold a meeting is, "Is it necessary that we have a meeting?" There are only four reasons to hold a meeting:

1   To make decisions,

2   to motivate a team or group,

3   to coordinate action or exchange information, or

4   to discuss problems or opportunities.

A meeting is an investment in time and money, and may result in possible lost productivity in other areas. Here are some points to consider before deciding whether to have a meeting. Would a memo, e-mail, or voice mail message be as effective as a meeting? If the answer is yes, don't have the meeting. If several people can get together informally to discuss and/or act on an issue in a few minutes, don't call a meeting. Don't hold meetings simply out of habit. Assess the continuing need for any regular meeting held more than once a month. What is the worst thing that might happen if we do not meet? What is the purpose of the meeting? How can we measure the meeting's success or value?

KEYS TO SUCCESSFUL MEETINGS

After you have asked these questions and realize that the answer is "Yes, we should have a meeting," follow the keys to successful meetings listed below. When you do hold a meeting require everyone to be prepared.

- Have a purpose, written agenda, and time budget for every meeting. Have a detailed written agenda in advance with location, time, length of meeting, and any preparation they need to make. The agenda should include a short description of the goals and expected outcomes, and should be distributed to all meeting participants in advance giving time to review, prepare, and discuss. How far in advance the written agenda is distributed should depend on the amount of preparation required by the participants before the meeting. Preparation prior to a meeting is vital to a successful meeting. The amount of preparation will vary with the topic and the expertise of the attendees. Increase the preparation time and decrease the meeting time!

- For a successful meeting to happen, the leader must be able to adapt leadership styles to different groups, different members and different tasks. The leader who uses the authoritarian style all of the time will fail!

- Invite only those who are needed and are essential to the success of the meeting's goals. Ask, who should participate and why? What is the best number of participants to reach resolution? Most people will be happy having one less meeting to go to, however some with easily offended egos may be upset unless you explain the objective criteria for attendance.

- Start meetings on time and end early or on time. Don't punish those who arrive on time by making them wait for those who don't. The person chairing the meeting is responsible for 1) leadership, 2) starting on time, 3) ending on time or ending early, and 4) where to hold the meeting. The facilitator should arrive early and make certain that the meeting room is set up properly. Tell the participants where they can find rest rooms, a coffee machine, telephones to use during breaks, and whatever else they may need. Review the agenda and reinforce the purpose of the meeting. Modify the agenda as needed to include last minute developments.

- Keep on track. A printed agenda will be a big help. Prioritize the agenda. Address A's first, then B's, and finally the C's (A's are the highest priority issues and C's the lowest priority). If you should run out of time during the meeting, you will have done the most important things (A's).

- When you're finished, quit! Adjourn the meeting when you have covered everything. Those who want to stay around and talk after the meeting can do so, and those who need to do other things can do so.

- Provide written action minutes after the meeting. Written minutes do the following: (1) document decisions made at the meeting, and (2) hold those with assignments from the meeting responsible for completing their assignments. After the meeting, prepare the minutes promptly. Distribute them as soon as possible. The minutes should include meeting date, time, place, purpose, names of attendees, conclusions, agreements, action items, and assignments. The minutes should not try to summarize the discussions or point out who said what.

- Don't allow interruptions if possible. If the subject is important enough to deserve a meeting, it should not be preempted by distractions. Avoid taking phone calls during meetings. Because you don't know who is calling you, you will give the impression that anyone calling you is more important than the person you are meeting with. Ground rules for participants should include turning off beepers and cell phones before entering the meeting.

- Try not to hold regularly scheduled meetings. If you hold a regularly scheduled meeting, re-determine on a regular basis if the meeting is really needed. If you have regular meetings, ask the group periodically "Do we still need this meeting at this frequency?". Often the answer is NO. Listen to what the group says. Exceptions include meetings required by the expectations of accrediting agencies, medical staff by laws, etc.

- Recap, summarize, and state conclusions at the end of the meeting. The facilitator should leave no issues unresolved and should review all decisions and commitments made. Issues not resolved during the meeting because of a need for additional information or the absence of a key stakeholder, etc., need to be addressed. This can be included in the action minutes. End the meeting on an upbeat note. An example is summarizing the progress made on the issues.

- Plan to end meetings or presentations ahead of schedule. The extra time provides flexibility to expand on a point or answer a question. Q&A should be part of almost every meeting. Allow for questions during the discussion of each agenda item. At some point you have to state that you must move ahead to the next agenda item. Look out for the obstructionists, the spinners, the passive-aggressors, and the snipers. If the extra time isn't needed, the audience will be pleasantly surprised by the early conclusion, and probably consider it a sign of efficiency and professionalism.

In order of frequency, specific meeting problems include: getting off the subject, no goals, no agenda, too lengthy, poor or inadequate preparation, inconclusiveness, and disorganized and ineffective leadership.

Try deciding things without a meeting. If someone calls and asks to get together, ask, "Can't we do it now on the phone?" Or, if a person stops you in the hall and wants to call a meeting, say, "Since we are already here together, let's just decide now." As appropriate, follow up with a written summary (could be e-mail) to ensure mutual understanding of what was discussed/decided. The success of a meeting is usually determined by the work done outside of the meeting, not by the number of meetings held.

THE PARTICIPANT'S ROLE

So far we have looked at skills of the meeting leader. It also takes skills to be an effective meeting participant. As a meeting participant you too have responsibilities. You should prepare for the meeting and then have something to offer. Be prepared to influence the group, keep on the subject, and help manage conflict if it arises. Make certain to ask for an agenda for the meeting if you have not received one in advance. Be a good listener at the meeting. Use good manners at the meeting by following The Golden Rule. Monitor your non-verbal signals, such as facial expressions, yawning, and doodling.

The next chapter addresses 33 time-wasters, plus ways you can control them.

Chapter 14

Thirty-Three Common Time-Wasters That Decrease Your Productivity

Time is our scarcest resource, and unless it is managed nothing else can be managed.

—Peter Drucker

You may plan your day each day and intend to have a productive time of it, but time wasters abound to throw you off the track. They include things such as negative influences from others, outmoded methods and tools, placing value on the worthless, and delays created by forces beyond your control. All of us have time-wasters that consume hours of our day. Getting control of your time-wasters is one of the best ways to start managing your time better. The following list includes most people's top time-wasters:

- Telephone interruptions
- Drop-in visitors
- Meetings
- Crisis management
- Lack of objectives
- Lack of priorities
- Lack of deadlines
- Cluttered desk
- Personal disorganization
- Ineffective delegation
- Attempting too much
- Unrealistic time estimates
- Confused responsibility
- Watching television
- Not having a place for things
- E-mail
- Procrastination
- Inability to say "no"
- Leaving tasks unfinished
- Lack of self discipline
- Junk mail
- Losing things
- Conflicting instructions
- Lack of a check list
- Long lunch hours
- Travel and driving time
- Day dreaming
- Excessive socializing
- Failure to perform tasks correctly
- Lack of clear communication
- Surfing the Internet
- Disorganized spouse
- Voice mail

Act now! Identify your top five time-wasters and record them on the chart on the next two pages. Then plan to take action to eliminate or control the time wasters that come at you in your life to give you more time for more important items.

Minimizing My Top Five Time-Wasters

1   **Time-Waster** _____

To minimize this time-waster I will:

1

2

3

4

2   **Time-Waster**_____

To minimize this time-waster I will:

1

2

3

4

3   **Time-Waster**_____

To minimize this time-waster I will:

1

2

3

4

4   **Time-Waster**_____

To minimize this time-waster I will:

1

2

3

4

5   **Time-Waster**_____

To minimize this time-waster I will:

1

2

3

4

CONTROLLING YOUR TIME-WASTERS

Here are some tips to help you control the time-wasters listed above.

Telephone Interruptions:

- Answer, "How can I help you?" rather than, "How are you?"

- When you're busy, let voice mail or another person answer your calls if it's appropriate.

- When a caller is too long-winded or calls when you are working on higher priorities, cut the person off politely and diplomatically by explaining that you have a time constraint, such as a meeting to attend or someone in your office, that prevents you from talking. Suggest a time when you'll be able to talk. Note: Use this tip only when it's appropriate and always tell the truth!

Inability to Say No:

If you have a reason for saying no, give the reason.

- Offer the person another way to meet his or her objective.

- Remember the four steps to saying no: listen, say no, give reasons, and offer alternatives.

Drop-in Visitors:

- When someone comes into your office, stand up and keep standing up. It's polite and will shorten the visitor's stay.

- Set a time limit at the outset. Say something like, "Sure, I can help you with that, but I've got to leave at 10:15."

- When someone drops in, say, "I need 15 minutes to wrap up this report. I'll come to your office then."

- Try working in an unused conference room, an empty office, the library, or the cafeteria before or after mealtimes. No one will know where you are, so you won't have drop-in visitors and other interruptions.

- When you see that a visit is going to go on longer than you expected, say, "Jim Bob, I thought this was going to be a short question. I should have asked you how long it was going to take. I have a 1:00 deadline to meet with my team leader. Can we reschedule this for tomorrow at 4:15?"

- Encourage appointments rather than unscheduled visits.

- Rearrange your furniture so that you aren't facing the door.

- Remove any extra chairs from your office.

- Close your door.

- Don't make unnecessary conversation.

- Keep a record of your interruptions, using the form in Chapter 9.

Leaving Tasks Unfinished:

- Prioritize the tasks on the to-do list in your datebook organizer.

- Work on "A" priorities first. That way you will have completed the important things on your list if you run out of time.

- Complete a task before putting it aside.

Meetings:

- Don't hold a meeting if a phone conversation will suffice.

- When you do hold a meeting, require everyone to be prepared.

- Have a written, prioritized agenda and stick to it.

- Start meetings on time and end on time or even early.

Lack of Self-Discipline:

- Have written goals and a plan for reaching them.

- Stick to your plan.

- Make a to-do list in your datebook organizer.

Crisis Management:

- Remember that it's much more efficient to head off problems before they develop.

- Expect the unexpected.

- Have a plan for everything that can go wrong.

- Have a priority list of important tasks that must be handled in advance.

- Focus on long-term plans and consequences whenever possible and defer tasks that only appear urgent on the surface.

- Learn to question the urgent and realize that many things only appear to need immediate attention.

Junk Mail:

- Open your mail over a large garbage can.

- Make junk mail a "D" priority.

- Don't handle junk mail more than once.

Lack of Objectives:

- Develop written goals.

- Develop objectives to serve as a plan for reaching your goals.

Losing Things:

- List the things you often have trouble finding.

- Write down where you plan to keep those items in the future and always put them in the places you have identified.

Lack of Priorities:

- Have a prioritized to-do list and stick to it.

- Prepare a to-do list in your datebook organizer at the end of each day.

Conflicting Instructions:

- Make certain that you are clear about what is expected of you when your manager delegates something to you.

- Make an extra effort to ensure that other people involved also understand what's expected.

- Summarize your understanding of the situation.

Lack of Deadlines:

- Set realistic deadlines for all items when you make your to-do list at the end of each day.

- Prioritize every item on your to-do list.

Cluttered Desk:

- A cluttered desk is an interruption every time you try to find something.

- Clear your desk.

- Have only the work you are currently doing on your desk, keeping other items somewhere else.

- Work on one task at a time to help yourself concentrate and think clearly.

Long Lunch Hours:

- Realize that time is money and that lost time is never found again. This might be the motivation you need to stop wasting time on long lunch hours.

Personal Disorganization:

- Schedule and prioritize everything you do.

- Realize that time is money and that lost time is never found again. This may be the motivation you need to stop wasting time on being disorganized.

Travel and Driving Time:

- Listen to motivational or educational audiotapes or CDs while you travel.

- Always have something with you to do while you travel.

- Remember that you do have some choice about where you live.

- Send someone else.

- Make sure you can't accomplish your purpose with a fax, letter, e-mail, phone call, or conference call.

- If possible, postpone a trip until you will be in the area anyway by suggesting, "I'll be in your area in three weeks. Can it wait until then?"

Ineffective Delegation:

- Train your team members to do more tasks that don't require your expertise.

- Don't permit "upward" delegation.

- Never take on a problem from someone who reports to you unless he or she has suggested a solution.

Daydreaming:

- Realize that time is your most priceless resource.

- Ask yourself whether daydreaming is going to help you accomplish any of your goals.

Attempting Too Much:

- Focus on what's really important.

- Don't work compulsively on unimportant tasks.

- Prioritize everything you do, then work on "A" priorities before "B"s, and so on.

- Be realistic about what you can really do.

Excessive Socializing:

- Realize that time is money and that lost time is never found again. This may be the motivation you need to stop wasting time on excessive socializing.

Unrealistic Time Estimates:

- Keep track of what you do in 15-minute time intervals for one week to get a better feel for how long things take.

Failure to Perform Tasks Correctly:

- Visualize yourself as a winner.

- Remember that successful people rarely make the same mistake twice.

- Have a back-up plan for when things go wrong.

Confused Responsibility:

- Be sure that you're clear about what's expected of you when your manager delegates something to you.

- Summarize often.

Lack of Clear Communication:

- Be sure that you're clear about what's expected of you when your manager delegates something to you.

- Summarize often.

- Make an extra effort to ensure that other people involved also understand what's expected.

Watching Television:

- Mark the programs you want to watch in the television schedule at the beginning of the week, the watch only those programs.

- Turn the television off as soon as the program is over, leaving the room to do something on your to-do list.

- Use your VCR to record the programs you want to watch, play them back at a convenient time, and fast forward through the commercials.

Surfing the Internet:

- Put practical limits, such as one or two hours a week, on your Internet-surfing time.

- Schedule your Internet-surfing time in your datebook organizer.

- Resist the temptation to waste time on the Internet, asking yourself whether what you're doing will put you closer to one of your high-priority goals.

Not Having a Place for Things:

- List the things you often have trouble finding.

- Write down where you plan to keep those items in the future and always put them in the places you have identified.

Disorganized Spouse:

- Share this book with your spouse and show him or her how it has helped you by "walking the talk."

- Obtain a videotape or DVD on time management from the library or one of the sources listed in Chapter 18, watch it together, and discuss how your spouse can use the information to get better organized.

E-Mail:

- Check e-mail several times each day. Don't become chained to e-mail by monitoring incoming e-mail on a continuous basis. E-mail creates its own sense of urgency, but most of the communications are not urgent. Constantly checking and responding to e-mail is like having letters delivered to your door one at a time. It's a big distraction and a poor use of your time. Let your incoming e-mail accumulate and respond to them several times per day.

- Get off unnecessary e-mail lists. The best way to deal with a problem is to never have it. If you are receiving lots of unwanted e-mails, ask to be removed from the various lists. This would include your inclusion in unwanted "cc" lists and unappreci-ated solicitations from those promising "unlimited wealth with-out risk or effort."

- Share you e-mail address only with those whom you want to give direct access. You might want to get a separate e-mail address that you use only for the important communications you wish to receive.

- As you open each e-mail do one of the following: (a) If it requires a quick response (for example, it will only take a minute or two), respond to it and delete it; (b) If it requires a response but is not the best use of your time, try to think of a way of delegating it; or, (c) If it is going to take any serious amount of time to respond (beyond a minute or two), schedule it for action in your datebook organizer and then download the message, save it, or print it out for future action.

- The first time you deal with a new prospect, always get their e-mail address. After one unsuccessful follow-up phone call (left message, but no return call), send them an e-mail. This usually gets a quick response. As a result, the length of the sales process is decreased drastically.

- When you are replying to an incoming message, if the subject has changed from the message originally sent you, change the subject! Don't just let the subject of your reply be "Re:" some topic that is no longer relevant. People like to know what an incoming message is really about. If you are answering a portion of the incoming message, copy that portion into your reply with indent marks (>) or brackets (<<>>) to identify it. Don't set your e-mail program to copy the entire message into the reply automatically. Copying an entire message should be done rarely.

Voice Mail:

- Record the message in your own voice and update it frequently with personal, informational messages. Don't say, "I'm not able to come to the phone right now," or "I'm either on the phone or away from my desk." That's obvious! The message should be accurate, brief, clear, and up to date. An outdated greeting shows a lack of concern. I change my message almost every day and some days the message is changed up to four times to better serve my clients.

- The recording should name an alternative person to speak to if the desired person isn't available.

- If you frequently check your voice-mail for messages, say so in your message. People want to know how long it will be before you get their messages.

- Make sure to change your message when you are out of town. You could lose an important client by not calling back for several days or even weeks.

- Return all calls or ask someone to return them on your behalf. Inform all key clients about your system, why you installed it, and how to use it. This is good customer service.

Procrastination:

- Clear the clutter.

- Establish an environment that is conducive to getting the job done.

- Use to-do lists effectively.

- Divide and conquer.

- Picture the end result of the finished job.

- Use the form in Chapter 12 to keep a record of what tasks you procrastinated on, why, and how you can minimize the problem next time.

The next chapter gives you numerous tips for increasing productivity through effective time management.

Chapter 15

Tips for Increasing Your Productivity Through Effective Time Management

People who make the worst use of their time are the same ones who complain that there is never enough time.

—Anonymous

Most time-saving ideas save only a few minutes a day, but those minutes add up to hours. A newly efficient person using the tips below should be able to save several hours a day—a significant amount of time. Reread these tips frequently for maximum benefit. And remember, the time you free up by using these time-management tips will be wasted unless you write down what you're going to do with the extra time.

DATEBOOK ORGANIZER (ELECTRONIC OR PAPER)

- Use your datebook organizer every day.

- Write essentially everything that you do in your datebook organizer along with your goals.

- Get rid of all your other calendars and use your datebook organizer instead.

- Keep your datebook organizer with you at all times.

- Make a to-do list in your datebook organizer at the end of every day, including your daily objectives, priorities, and time estimates rather than just random activities.

- Plan your time by writing out plans for each day and week in your datebook organizer.

- Remember that the best time-management system is an integrated one that allows you to retrieve information, track projects, focus on your goals, and record key decisions.

DELEGATING

- Keep a delegation log and use it to jot down details whenever you delegate an assignment so that you'll be able to monitor progress and take appropriate action when necessary.

- Select people who are able to do the job.

- Stress that you are more concerned about the project's final outcome than day-to-day details as the project progresses.

FILES

- Set up a tickler file, a system for filing papers you want to have reappear on specific dates. Label folders one through 31 for each day of the month, plus 12 additional folders for each month of the year. Every day you pull out that day's file folder and take action on its contents. On the first day of the month, you also pull out the month file. For example, if today is the third day of the month and you want to follow up on a proposal in 10 days, you would put a copy of the proposal and associated information in the "13" file.

- Create an idea file, where you can file interesting items with dated notes saying why you found them interesting. Go through the file each month. Toss out ideas you will never use and act on others. Toss out any item that's still there after six months, because you will never get to it.

- Create additional referral folders for a handful of people you talk to regularly. If you've got something to discuss with someone, put it in his or her file and take action when it's convenient.

- Void the "miscellaneous" category in your files. Make yourself come up with some association for the file name. Miscellaneous is a synonym for meaningless.

- Keep everything filed except the one item you are working on right now.

- Don't let magazines and newspapers pile up. Clip what you need and establish files for clippings. Discard the rest.

- A computer hard drive is an electronic filing cabinet! If you continue to add more and more files and software programs without deleting the ones you no longer need or use, the hard drive, like your file drawers, will eventually become stuffed to capacity.

- Other items you can toss include manuals for equipment you no longer use, lapsed insurance policies, old bank statements, payment schedules for loans you've repaid, expired warranties, and miscellaneous canceled checks used for purchases that weren't tax deductible.

GOALS

- Have goals and a plan for reaching them.

- Re-examine your goals every few months to make certain you're on the right track.

- Be realistic about saying yes to someone who wants your time. A person who has no goals is often used by someone who does.

INTERRUPTIONS

- Develop a strategy for avoiding and handling interruptions.

- Plan interruptions away from priority times when possible.

- Keep a record of interruptions, including who interrupted you, why, and how to reduce this interruption in the future.

- Eliminate interruptions temporarily by posting a sign on your office door that says, "Please do not disturb between 10:00 and 11:00 a.m. Leave your phone number and a message that you dropped by, and I'll call you between 11:00 a.m. and noon today."

- People who can't say no will always be at the mercy of drop-in visitors, telephone interruptions, and "upward" delegation.

MEETINGS

- Meetings should have a written agenda and action minutes.

- Meetings should start on time and end on time or even early.

- Plan to end meetings or presentations ahead of schedule. The extra time gives you the flexibility you need to expand on a point or answer a question. If the extra time isn't needed, the audience will be pleasantly surprised by the early conclusion. They'll probably consider it a sign of efficiency and professionalism.

- Only invite people who really need to be at the meeting.

- The only four reasons to hold a meeting are to make decisions, to motivate a team or group, to coordinate action or exchange information, or to discuss problems or opportunities.

- If you have regular meetings, ask the group whether you still need to meet that regularly. The answer is often no. Listen to what the group says.

- Make meetings more effective by holding them only when a conference call, e-mail, voice mail, or memo won't accomplish the goal.

- Try deciding things without a meeting. If someone calls and asks to get together, ask, "Can't we do it on the phone right now?" Or if a person stops you in the hall and wants to call a meeting, say, "Since we are already here together, let's just decide now."

- As a meeting participant, your responsibilities include preparing for the meeting, having something to offer, being prepared to influence the group, keeping on the subject, and helping manage conflict if it arises.

- Recap, summarize, and state conclusions at the end of the meeting.

DESK AND OFFICE ORGANIZATION

- Avoid clutter. Keep everything you are not working on out of your immediate work area.

- Clean off your desk just before leaving your office each day.

- Have the things you use frequently right at your fingertips.

- Angle your desk away from open doorways, busy corridors, or windows, which are all sources of distraction.

- Dispose of desk clutter by eliminating dispensable items such as photos, gadgets, and magazines. Put these items on a bookshelf in the office.

PAPERWORK

- Whenever possible, handle papers only once. When that isn't possible, put a check mark on the paper's top corner each time you handle it. When you see three checks marks, ask yourself why you aren't taking action on this piece of paper. You may be procrastinating.

- If the paper in your hands duplicates information you have or could easily obtain elsewhere, has no tax implications, and is of no apparent use to you, get it off your desk and out of your files. Put it in a recycling bin!

- To decrease the time and expenses involved with photocopy distribution, trim the distribution list and see whether anyone who gets dropped asks for the material.

- To decrease the time and expenses involved with photocopy distribution, attach notes asking recipients if they would rather receive the information by e-mail.

- To decrease the time and expenses involved with photocopy distribution, make one copy for each department and ask them to route it internally.

- Write responses to in-house memos and letters in the margins and send the originals back to the sender. You'll save extra time by not having to file a copy.

- You can quickly customize computerized form letters for each recipient. Keep a file of form letters on your computer hard drive for announcements, confirmations, thank-yous, and so on.

PLANNING

- Set a deadline for every task.

- Schedule some open time to give yourself some flexibility every day.

- Schedule work for the time of the day that's best-suited for the type of work you'll be doing.

- Have a plan for every day.

- Expect the unexpected! Have a back-up plan for things that can go wrong.

- Schedule your time each day to make sure that you accomplish the most important things first. Allow flexibility for the unexpected, such as interruptions.

- Adapt the philosophy that lack of prior planning on someone else's part does not constitute an emergency on your part.

- Prioritize work according to your body clock. Once you have determined when you are at your personal best, institute personal flextime and schedule tough tasks for those times. Schedule repetitive jobs for times when your body clock is winding down.

- The more you plan, the more you do.

- Consider scheduling a meeting with yourself to plan, organize your files, organize your desk, or finish a project.

- Stay organized by keeping current on all your incoming correspondence, whether paper or electronic. Prioritize mail and be decisive about filing it or throwing it away.

- A daily written plan is the single most effective time-management strategy, yet only one person in ten does it! The other nine go home muttering, "Where did the day go?"

- You can't predict when a crisis will occur, but careful planning can alleviate the problem when it does occur. Expect the unexpected!

- Schedule tasks that require others' actions for early in the day. By reaching people early, you're more likely to get them to do what you need that day.

- Prioritize by imagining that you are leaving town for a month starting tomorrow. What four things would you absolutely have to finish before you left? Try the same trick tomorrow and the next day and the next....

- Make Mondays easier by using the last hour on Fridays to straighten your desk and office and set up a couple of easy assignments for Monday morning. This allows you to get off to a fast start after the weekend.

- When you are working on an "A" priority and don't want to be interrupted, put a sign on your door that says, "I will get back to you after 3:00 p.m. today. Leave a message with (insert name) if you want me to call you back."

- Use a checklist for recurring activities. For example, if you travel often, keep a list of all the things you need on trips in your date-book organizer, suitcase, or lap-top computer.

ATTENDING SEMINARS, WORKSHOPS, AND PROFESSIONAL MEETINGS

- Prepare ahead of time. Make a list of questions you want answered, for example. Or make a list of people with whom you want to talk and network.

- Use breaks to network with your peers. This is a great time to make lunch and dinner plans so you can talk with a lot of different people.

- Collect handouts from as many speakers as possible, even those whose sessions you don't attend.

- Take notes on the handouts and review them on your way home. Use a highlighter to emphasize the important points.

- Conduct a mini-seminar on the key points for your co-workers or team members when you get back to work.

- Don't let notes from important seminars, workshops, or meetings get stuck in a file out of sight and out of mind. During your return travel or first thing back at the office, go over your notes and highlight actions you want to take. Write them in your datebook organizer.

TECHNOLOGY

- Use technology to get things done, when appropriate. Try computers, fax machines, modems, audiocassette players and recorders, CD players, cellular phones, voice mail, e-mail, VCRs, and so on.

- Before purchasing new computer software, ask yourself whether it's better than a pencil. The answer will help you decide if the expense is justified. Keep in mind that a computer is supposed to make your work easier and faster.

- Don't keep inefficient, slow, and antiquated technology when reliable and faster technology is available.

- Back up computer files daily. According to a 3M Company report in the *Wall Street Journal*, almost a third of all business users of PCs lose data each year. They spend an average of one week to reconstruct or recover information. Nationwide this amounts to 24 million business days a year, valued at about $4 billion.

- Find out how much space is available on your computer hard drive. If you have a 200-megabyte drive with 18 megabytes available, your drive is 91 percent full. It's time to start taking action when your drive is more than 75 percent full. When your drive is too full, you start running out of room to store information. Your computer also runs slower, because software programs need additional room to store the temporary and back-up files they are always making. If there's too little room, processing slows down.

- Keep your computer hard-drive desegmented and "healthy."

- The cassette or CD player in your car can have a major impact on your life. Tapes and CDs can get you pumped up and ready for action. You can also learn a lot! Check your library for audio-tapes and CDs that interest you.

- Eliminate communication errors and save time by taking advantage of voice mail.

- A lap-top computer can help you get work accomplished in airplanes, motel rooms, and other places.

- Use a dictation device rather than a secretary using shorthand.

- When used correctly, voice mail and e-mail can eliminate time-wasting telephone tag.

- Speaker-phones allow you to talk to people without holding the phone, which frees you to do other things while you talk.

- Routine tasks can be handled by technology. Let your employer deposit your paycheck for you. Use electronic pay for utility bills and any other companies that are set up for receiving electronic payments. Computer programs such as Quicken will allow you to use this service.

TELEPHONES

- Return phone calls from 11:30 a.m. to noon and 4:30 to 5:00 p.m. The people you call will keep their conversations shorter, especially on Friday afternoons.

- Let people you deal with often know when you are available to receive calls and when you aren't. This will help you avoid telephone-tag problems.

- Jot key points down in your datebook organizer before making a phone call.

- To get through to someone who is not returning your phone calls, fill out a standard telephone message slip and fax it to the person. Your message will stand out among the others.

- To minimize telephone tag, ask the other person's secretary when the best time to call is.

- Control your phone use. Don't let the telephone control you.

- Take notes before and during phone calls so you'll remember important items to discuss.

- Look into time-saving products and services from your local phone company.

- Just because your home phone is ringing doesn't mean that you have to stop what you're doing to answer it. If you are doing something with a high priority, let the phone ring or let your voice mail pick it up. If the call is really important, the person will call again or leave a voice mail message.

- Try limiting your phone calls to three minutes by placing an egg timer by your telephone. You won't think this is silly when you see how well it works!

- If you keep missing calls, leave a message that says, "I am easiest to reach between 1:00 and 3:00 p.m. Central Time. Give the same call-back time for all of your calls.

- Make sure the next telephone you purchase is headset compatible. If you use your phone a lot, you'll find a headset really increases your productivity.

- Reach decision-makers by calling before 7:45 or 8:45 in the morning. This "oldie" still works. Secretaries normally arrive at 8:00 or 9:00, while their bosses often get to the office an hour earlier. If the phone rings, chances are that they will answer personally. Find out what time the business officially opens and call 15 to 30 minutes earlier.

- Keep your list of phone and fax numbers up to date so that you reach the party without having to try again with a different number.

- Use voice mail when you don't want to be disturbed. Include in the voice-mail message when you will be able to return calls.

- Schedule a telephone hour to return all calls.

- Obtain and record the number for the direct line to anyone you need to call again.

TRAVEL

- Have something to do with you at all times.

- Remember that flights scheduled early in the day are usually less likely to be delayed than later ones. That's because airlines schedule flights so tightly and leave so little turn-around time that a single delay can cause a chain reaction for all later flights.

- When booking a flight, ask the reservation clerk for information about on-time performance for that specific flight. Displayed on the computer screen, those data are readily available to customers.

- To prevent jet lag when traveling across several time zones, go to bed two hours earlier when traveling east and two hours later when traveling west for several nights before your trip.

- If your flight is cancelled after you arrive at the airport, find the nearest phone, call the airline's reservation number, and ask to be rebooked on the next scheduled flight to your destination. This lets you avoid waiting in long lines with other passengers trying to rebook.

- In one hour of flight time, you can often accomplish what would take you three hours of normal time in the office.

- When you return from a trip, immediately deal with to-do list items associated with the trip, such as expense reports, letters to prospective clients you met on the trip, ideas you collected, and so forth. If you procrastinate, you will have forgotten the details by the time you get to it and won't be able to capitalize on the value of the trip.

- Make your briefcase into a traveling desk. Carry file folders labeled "File," "Act," "Call," "Calls Expected," "Computer," and "Entry." In the upper-right corner of your "Act" file, indicate the specific action you need to take.

- Always have something to do when waiting to board a plane or see someone for an appointment. You'll be motivated to read it so that you can lighten your briefcase.

- In your computer, keep a file of directions to various places. When you want to return to a friend's house, meeting place, or anywhere else, retrieve the directions from your file rather than wasting time asking for them again.

- Make a copy of your paper airline ticket for easier replacement it it's lost or stolen. If you travel out of the country, make copies of your passport pages that bear the passport number. Make copies of your credit cards.

MISCELLANEOUS TIPS

- Make sure that the first hour of every day is a productive hour. Get off to a good start.

- Keep a time log for one to two weeks occasionally to help you analyze how you are really using your time. This will help you keep bad habits out of your life.

- Tackle the work that you like doing the least during your high-energy times. For most people, that means mornings.

- Don't spend more time being organized than you do getting work done.

- Don't confuse activity with accomplishment.

- Always be looking for ways to work smarter, not harder.

- You can become very knowledgeable about something brand-new in six months if you spend an hour each day learning that new topic! Every hour is important. Try to get a little better every day.

- Ask people who report to you to bring you solutions, not just problems.

- Schedule quiet time to get things done.

- Learn to say no diplomatically and effectively. Learn to decline tactfully but firmly every request that does not contribute to your goals and overall plan.

- Efficiency means doing the job right, but effectiveness means doing the right job efficiently. Work on the right things!

- Remember Pareto's Law: You can accomplish 80 percent of your objectives each day if you work on the right 20 percent.

- Dedicate each week to eliminating one of your time-wasters.

- Limit television-viewing.

- Think about the following questions carefully: "What am I doing that someone else can do?" "What am I doing that really does not need to be done at all?" and "What will happen if this is not done at all?"

- Do every job right the first time.

- Avoid the many activity traps you encounter. Focus on results, not just activities.

- Get the amount of sleep you need, but no more than really necessary.

- Rise early in the morning.

- Pop out of bed as soon as you wake rather than lingering under the covers. One incentive is to think of the most pleasant activity on your day's to-do list.

- Be a good listener.

- Break large tasks into smaller tasks. Divide and conquer.

- Increase your reading speed.

- Decide what to wear tomorrow before you go to sleep tonight. Preparing early ensures that all your clothes are properly cleaned, ironed, and mended. It also saves precious time. You'll begin the day in better control of yourself and with a more positive outlook.

- Stop smoking! The average smoker spends several hours a week buying cigarettes, flicking ashes, smoking without doing any-thing else, snuffing cigarettes out, and emptying ashtrays. Smokers are sick more frequently than non-smokers. When you're sick, you can't practice good time management. According to one estimate, each cigarette you smoke shortens your life by approximately 18 minutes! And those who smoke and drive have more automobile accidents than those who don't.

- Don't be afraid to reschedule because of interruptions and crises. It's better than being late, and others will appreciate your concern.

- Show by example how time-management principles make work much easier when used properly and consistently. If you do this enough, some of your co-workers will become interested. Share with others what you have learned from this book. Be a good example!

- Encourage everyone you work with to help each other with chronic time-wasting problems.

- Subscribe to selective newsletters. Many successful, busy people rely on editors to select the most important news items, facts, and breakthroughs for them.

- Reserve one place in your home and office to put things that need to be taken with you when you leave. Check this "take-away" spot as you are getting ready to leave. That way you won't forget to take something important with you.

- Avoid the sales rep's number-one time-waster: taking the rest of the day off after a big sale. A better approach is to take advantage of your positive momentum to build on your success.

- Spend time like money and recognize that you only have a limited supply. Use it to do what is important to you—your goals—not what others say is important.

- Start improving your time-management skills by working on one aspect of time management each month. Start with the biggest time-waster.

- Don't waste time reading items that offer no benefit to your personal or professional life.

- List all the tasks you do in a typical week or month and determine which ones could have been handled by an outside service or an assistant.

- Boost your creativity and productivity by spending time with people who are successful in fields other than your own. It's amazing how many creative ideas can be found by observing innovative practices in other industries and adapting them to your own.

- Learn and practice ways to process information quickly and decisively.

- Unlearning old habits and learning new ones are difficult yet essential steps toward effective time management.

- "No" is the most powerful time-saving word in the English language. The four steps to saying no are listening, saying no, giving reasons, and offering alternatives.

- Being indecisive is a big time-waster.

- By not managing your time effectively, you deny yourself the opportunity to do outstanding work.

- Remember why you wanted to manage your time better. Would you like to get more done, work smarter but not harder, spend more time with your family, or save time for working out?

- Crisis management means dealing with a crisis after it occurs. The best way to handle a crisis is to keep it from happening in the first place. Make plans to prevent crises or reduce their impact.

- To help prevent crisis management, get into the habit of asking, "What could go wrong?" "What else could go wrong?" "And what else?" Expect the unexpected!

- Before reading something, ask, "Is this likely to move me toward my high-priority goals?" If not, maybe you shouldn't read it.

- Be a contrarian at least some of the time. Do things when no one else is doing them. For example, check out of your hotel while others are still in bed. Use the photocopier or printer while everyone else is at lunch. Eat at restaurants before or after the big rush.

- Find the time of day when you work at your peak. All of us have certain times when we do better work than at other times.

- Beware of Parkinson's Law, which says, "Work expands to fill the time available for its completion." Don't confuse activity with accomplishment. Efficiency is doing the right job, but effectiveness is doing the right job efficiently. Strive to be effective.

- Discipline yourself so that bad days don't turn into total wash-outs.

- Doing it now is the best method of handling the most unpleasant tasks, such as meetings you are dreading or phone calls you think will be unpleasant.

- Don't be penny wise and time foolish! Examples include keeping slow, inefficient technology when more reliable and faster models are available, using an airport shuttle that makes numerous stops before your destination instead of using a taxi, or living far away from your office just to save money.

- Continually ask yourself, "What for?" "Why am I doing it this way?" Think and work outside the box!

- Keep your list of addresses and e-mail addresses up to date, so that your mail doesn't get returned, delayed, or lost forever.

- One day every year, such as New Year's Day, change all the clock and smoke detector batteries in your home and office. Don't forget the batteries in your travel alarm clock! Most of the batteries for clocks and smoke detectors last slightly over one year. From a time-management standpoint it's best to change the batteries all at once before they run down.

- Put a price-tag on each hour of your time.

- Do you often misplace your claim checks for airport parking, shoe repair, dry cleaning, photo-developing, and so on? Carry them in your wallet. This also works well for movie and show tickets.

- Have you ever left your doctor's office and later recalled questions that you forgot to ask? Before your appointment, write a list of your concerns and add to it when another question comes to mind.

- When you purchase a new piece of equipment, complete your warranty card promptly and file a copy with the receipt attached in a convenient file.

- Carry an extra car key and house key in your wallet.

- A good attitude will save you time. Think positively! It's a big timesaver.

- Know when to ask for help. You can't always fix things, solve a problem, or find an answer by yourself. Save time by calling an expert.

- Increase your reading speed by taking a speed-reading course "live" or on cassette or CD. Set some speed-reading goals for yourself.

- Always read a book with a pen and highlighter in hand. Underlining and writing in the margins enhances the information value of a book. Then when you want to relook at the information, only study the notes, and what's underlined and highlighted.

- When working with a new hire, know when to cut your losses if the person is not working out.

- Know when to leave well enough alone.

- Become decisive. Knowing how to decide when to cut your losses or leave well enough alone is part of the part of the larger process of knowing how to make good decisions.

- Don't finish every book that you start. Know when to cut your losses and don't do things that are not worth doing.

- Put your name, address, phone number, and e-mail address on valuable items. And offer a reward.

- Use cues and reminders. In my electronic datebook or on the parking ticket, I always write the level and row I park in at the airport garage.

- Complain only to someone who can do something about your complaint. A well-timed and skillfully executed complaint can frequently give good results. Try to keep emotion out of the complaint. Have your facts handy. Keep a record of whom you talked to and when, and what was promised.

- Don't wait until it breaks to fix it. Perform preventative maintenance as appropriate.

- Find something you love to do and do it.

The next chapter is what you've all been waiting for: your 30-day plan for freeing up several hours a day.

Chapter 16

A 30-Day Plan for Freeing Up Two Hours a Day

Time is everything. Anything you accomplish—pleasure, success, fortune—is measured in time.

—Joyce C. Hall

Here's your 30-day plan for freeing up significant amounts of time. Participants in my time-management seminars and workshops who try the 30-day program free an average of 2.1 hours a day or 766 hours a year. While some free as little as 30 minutes a day or 182 hours a year, others free as much as four hours a day or 1,460 hours a year.

TODAY:

- Identify your top five time-wasters by looking at the list in Chapter 14.

- On the list in Chapter 14 where you have recorded your top five time-wasters, specify how you will minimize each time-waster. Use ideas from Chapters 14 and 15 of this book.

- Purchase and start using a datebook organizer (electronic or paper).

- Start setting goals for the next year or so.

FOR THE NEXT 21 DAYS:

- Work to eliminate or minimize three of your top five time-wasters using ideas from this book, the resources listed in Chapter 18, and my audiocassette *Increasing Productivity Through Effective Time Management*. Remember, it takes 21 days to build a pattern in your life.

- Finish setting your goals.

- Review Chapters 3 through 13

EVERY DAY:

- Use your datebook organizer.

- Write essentially everything you do in your datebook organizer.

- Make a to-do list in your datebook organizer at the end of each day.

- Review your goals.

DAYS 22–30:

- Start working to eliminate your other two top five time-wasters.

- Continue working to eliminate any of your first three time-wasters.

At the end of 30 days, you will have extra time! How many hours did you free up by having goals, having a plan to reach your goals, and following the suggestions and ideas presented in this book? Let me know. I am interested in you succeeding and being a winner! If you contact me using the contact information at the beginning of this book, I will enter your information in the database I use to keep track of how much time people are freeing up for other things.

USING YOUR EXTRA TIME

How will you use the extra time that you create? You'll probably waste the time if you don't write down what you plan to do with it.

Try reading more. In today's rapidly changing world, staying current is increasingly important. Having more time will let you read more and help you stay up-to-date, study new subjects, or learn more about something you already know. Investing in yourself is a great use of your extra time. Some ways you can invest in yourself include:

- Learning how to use your computer software so that it does more than just the basics

- Learning to speak another language

- Attending conferences and workshops

- Taking a night course at a local college in a subject you have always been interested in, but never had time to pursue

- Initiating or improving personal relationships

- Taking on new work projects

- Improving self-management skills, such as managing stress, time, or change, negotiating, leadership, or listening

- Starting or expanding a hobby

- Developing a new career

- Planning

- Beginning or expanding an exercise program

- Spending more time with your family

- Spending more time with your friends

Or just relax. You need some leisure time to stay healthy, both mentally and physically. When you don't take time off, you burn out. If you have too much bad stress in your life, you'll get sick. If you get sick, you won't be able to practice effective time-management. And effective time-management is what you need to achieve your goals.

The next chapter contains my favorite time management quotes.

Chapter 17
Useful Time Management Quotes

A short pencil is better than a long memory.

—Traditional saying

You may not be able to control the situation, but you can always control your reaction.

—Austin McGonigle

I run my life with motivational quotes. I find that they keep me on target. I use lots of quotes (with credit given) in my keynotes, seminars, and workshops. I have listed my favorite quotes in this chapter for your use. I hope that you find them as useful as I have.

Wasting just one hour a day means in 10 years you will have lost 3,650 hours or 152 days of your life. Every hour is important.
—Chris Frings

Hire for attitude and train for skill.
—Southwest Airlines hiring policy

Today is the first day of the rest of your life.
—Paul "Bear" Bryant

A bend in the road is not the end of the road unless you fail to make the turn.
—Author unknown

A cluttered desk is postponed decisions.
—Author unknown

The dinosaur doesn't exist today because it could not change and could not adapt— so it became extinct. We will become extinct soon if we can't change and adapt.
—Chris Frings

It's the itsy-bitsy teeny-weeny things that beat you.
—Paul "Bear" Bryant

Skills are like tax deductions; we use them or lose them.
—Chris Frings

The most important piece of plastic in your wallet is your library card. Use it frequently to check out audiotapes, videotapes, and books. Listen to instructional and motivational audiotapes while driving.
—Chris Frings

Get your priorities straight and have goals that put balance in your life. No one who is retired ever wished that he or she had spent more time at the office, returned more phone calls, or attended more meetings.
—Chris Frings

We must continually evaluate the value of all of our efforts.
—Author unknown

The more that you read, the more things you will know. The more that you learn, the more places you'll go.
—Dr. Seuss

Procrastination is opportunity's natural assassin.
—Victor Kiam

I've always been in the right place at the right time. Of course, I steered myself there.
—Bob Hope

Never use any computer software who's version number ends in 'point zero'!
—Dan Garrett

Life is what happens when you are busy making other plans.
—John Lennon

Nothing is less productive than to make more efficient what should not be done at all.
—Peter Drucker

When you make a mistake, there are only three things you should ever do about it: admit it, learn from it, and don't repeat it.
—Paul "Bear" Bryant

Once a task has begun,
Never leave it until it's done.
Though the task be great or small,
Do it right or not at all.
—Author unknown

If you can't define IT, you can't do IT.
—Thom Winninger, Professional speaker

Invest in yourself. It will pay you the rest of your life.
—Author unknown

People who make the worst use of their time are the same ones who complain that there is never enough time.
—Author unknown

Companies should spend less time projecting financial data from employees and more time teaching them to analyze and act on it.
—Bill Gates

Even if you're on the right track, you'll get run over if you just sit there.
—Will Rogers

Always do your best. What you plant now, you will harvest later.
—Og Mandino

A goal not in writing is a wish or a dream—it probably won't happen. A goal is a dream with a deadline. Goals are vehicles to make our dreams come true.
—Author unknown

If anything is worth doing at all, it is worth doing right.
—My Mother

Sign on a wall in a conference room: A meeting is no substitute for progress.
—Author unknown

We must have long-range goals to keep us from being frustrated by short-range failures.
—Author unknown

I don't know the key to success, but the key to failure is trying to please everybody.
—Bill Cosby

Shared goals build unity. Goal "setting" is important. Goal "doing" is more important. Writing a goal clarifies a goal.
—Author unknown

Abraham Lincoln was a great man, not because he once lived in a log cabin, but because his goals got him out of it.
—Author unknown

No matter how busy you are, you must take time to make other people feel important.
—Mary Kay Ash

Goals give direction, purpose and meaning to life.
—Author unknown

If you ONLY do what you used to do, you will get left out.
—Lawrence M. Killingsworth

If everyone is thinking alike then somebody isn't thinking.
—General George Patton

Expect the unexpected. Have a plan for everything that can go wrong. Have a plan and stick to your plan. Rehearse the things that can go wrong. Then when it happens you will have done it before and you will know how to handle the problem.
—Paul "Bear" Bryant

With respect to goals: A thing is not a thing until it's a thing. The main thing is to keep the main thing the main thing.
—Author unknown

The ten most powerful two letter words in the English dictionary are: if it is to be it is up to me.
—Author unknown

You can't get to second base and keep one foot on first base. A turtle doesn't move until he sticks his neck out.
—Author unknown

Only your best is good enough.
—My Mother

Eighty percent of the value is from twenty percent of the effort.
—Paredo, Italian economist

There is no right way to do a wrong thing.
—Ken Blanchard

If you fail to plan, you plan to fail.
—Author unknown

The main thing is to keep the main thing the main thing.
—Author unknown

You are never going to make it as a wandering generality. You have got to become a meaningful specific.
—Zig Ziglar